Ten-Minute Plays
VOLUME IX
FOR TEENS: DRAMA
10+ Format

Ten-Minute Plays

VOLUME IX

FOR TEENS

• • •

DRAMA

10+ Format

YOUNG ACTORS SERIES

Kristen Dabrowski

A Smith and Kraus Book

A Smith and Kraus Book
Published by Smith and Kraus, Inc.
177 Lyme Road, Hanover, NH 03755
www.SmithandKraus.com

© 2006 by Kristen Dabrowski
All rights reserved.

First Edition: April 2006
10 9 8 7 6 5 4 3 2 1
Manufactured in the United States of America

Cover and text design by Julia Hill Gignoux, Freedom Hill Design

ISBN 1-57525-440-9
10-Minute Plays for Kids Series ISSN 1553-0477

CONTENTS

TO THOMAS HARDY AND NICKY SILVER
two very different authors, but equally inspiring

INTRODUCTION

Ten-Minute Plays aims to score on many playing fields. This book contains twelve short plays. Each play then contains two scenes and four monologues. Add it up! That means that this book contains twelve plays, twenty-four scenes, and forty-eight monologues. There's a lot to choose from, but it's not overwhelming. The plays and scenes are marked clearly. Note that the text for the monologues is set in a different typeface. If you are working on a monologue and are not performing the play or scene as a whole, take the time to hear in your mind any additional lines or character responses that you need for the monologue to make sense.

Beat indicates there is a dramatic pause in the action. You will want to consider why the beat is there. Does no one know what to do? Is someone thinking?

Feel free to combine characters (so fewer actors are needed), change a character from male to female (or vice versa), or alter the text in any way that suits you. Be as creative as you like!

For each play, I've included tips for young actors and ideas for playwrights. Here's a guide to the symbols:

    😎 = tips for actors

    ✍ = ideas for playwrights

There's a lot to work with here. Actors, the tips are meant to give you some guidance and information on how to be an even finer actor. Playwrights, I've included a few of my inspirations and invite you to borrow from them to write your own plays.

At the end of each play is a section called "Talk Back!" with discussion questions. These questions are catalysts for class discussions and projects. The plays do not make moral judgments. They are intended to spark students to use their imaginations and create their own code of ethics. Even if you're not in school, "Talk Back!" can give you some additional ideas and interesting subjects to discuss.

Lastly, there are four extras in the Appendix: Character Questionnaire for Actors, Playwright's Checklist, Scene Elements Worksheet, and Exploration Games. Each activity adds dimension and depth to the plays and is intended to appeal to various learning styles.

Enjoy!

Kristen Dabrowski

CATHY

3F, 3M

WHO

FEMALES	MALES
Cathy	Rick
Gina	Russ
Meg	Ty

WHERE Scene 1: Russ's bedroom, night; Scene 2: Outside school, day.

WHEN Present day.

For this piece, you want to feel emotional, but then work to mask those feelings. We often do this in real life because we don't want people to see we're upset. These characters are no different.

This play was inspired by a tiny moment in the book *Wuthering Heights*. The final product does not relate to that incident at all, really, but see if you can choose a single moment from a book and build an entirely new play around it.

Scene 1: Visitation

(There is a tap at the window.)

RUSS: Who is it? *(A tap at the window.)* Who's there? *(Beat.)* Just the wind. *(A tap at the window.)* What is that? I'm trying to sleep. Whatever you are, go away! *(A tap at the window.)* What's going on? Who is that?

CATHY: Cathy!

RUSS: All right! All right! This had better be good!

(RUSS opens the window, and CATHY comes in.)

RUSS: What do you want?

CATHY: Want?

RUSS: What are you doing here? It's the middle of the night.

CATHY: I thought you'd be happy to see me.

RUSS: I was trying to sleep.

CATHY: Sorry.

RUSS: So what do you want?

CATHY: Nothing really. I just wanted to see someone.

RUSS: Well, now you see me.

CATHY: Right. *(Beat.)* Russ, I just wanted to see some-one. Can you understand that at all?

RUSS: I guess. But it's three A.M. I just don't get why it couldn't wait until tomorrow.

CATHY: It just couldn't. I needed to see someone now, and I thought of you. I thought you wouldn't mind. But you do.

RUSS: Not exactly. It's just that I'm tired, Cathy. It's nothing personal. Is something wrong? You're acting a little weird.

CATHY: Wrong? No. Nothing's wrong. Not exactly. Not completely. *(Beat.)* Yes. But I can't put a name on it. I don't know if I can say . . . I'm just . . . tired, Russ. And not like you are. In another way. I'm just sick and tired. I just feel . . . really alone and I wanted to be with someone. I just wanted to have another person to be around. Being at home with my family is like being alone. I don't know how to describe it. I just feel so empty and I thought maybe it would be different here. That I would feel less . . . cold or some-thing. It's hard to describe. I guess you don't un-derstand. I was just sitting in my room and all I could hear was the wind howling and it just filled me with such . . . . sadness. I was so unbearably sad. I just couldn't take it anymore. So I came here. I'm sorry I did. I didn't mean to bother you. I'll go now.

RUSS: Don't go. It's OK.

CATHY: You don't understand. And I didn't mean to

bother you. I just wanted—I didn't want to bother you. I'll let you sleep.

RUSS: No, stay. It's OK.

CATHY: Do you know what I mean, Russ? At all?

RUSS: A little maybe. I think maybe I do.

CATHY: You don't. I can tell. But that's good. I'm glad you don't feel like this. It's not a good feeling.

RUSS: Cath, I just don't know what to say to you.

CATHY: I know. But you don't have to say anything. It's OK.

RUSS: But I want to say the right thing. I feel like I need to say the right thing.

CATHY: But that's just it. My parents have been trying so hard to say the right thing, but there's nothing I need to hear, maybe. Words just don't matter.

RUSS: So what does matter?

CATHY: I just feel like I need a connection. It doesn't make any sense. I don't know.

RUSS: Would a hug help?

CATHY: I think so.

(RUSS hugs CATHY.)

RUSS: Any better?

CATHY: Sure.

RUSS: You're lying.

CATHY: No. I mean, I'm not better completely, but I do feel better. I just wish you didn't feel like you *had* to do that.

RUSS: I don't—

CATHY: No, don't feel bad. I bullied you into it. You feel sorry for me. I don't blame you. It's nice that you feel that way. I appreciate it.

RUSS: Seriously, Cath, I'm not being fake here. I just don't know what to say or do to make you feel better. Plus, I'm half asleep. I just feel like I have to say the right thing for some reason. This feels important. It is, isn't it? I don't know why you can't see yourself . . . You could go to a lot of people in the middle of the night. I'm not saying you shouldn't have come here, I'm glad you did, but a lot of people would have let you in. I'm sorry if I was being obnoxious at first; I didn't know it was you. But you shouldn't feel alone. You shouldn't feel disconnected. You shouldn't be sitting alone at three A.M. listening to the wind. Seriously, Cath. I wish I knew why you're so sad. Did someone do something to you? Did something happen? And is there something I can do? What should I do? What should I say here? Because whatever it is, I want to do it. I just have no idea what it is I'm supposed to do or say here. Seriously, just tell me.

CATHY: I don't know what to tell you. What you're

doing is right. I just needed to see someone. To be in the room with someone other than me.

RUSS: So did something happen to you?

CATHY: No. No. It's all me. There's something wrong with me.

RUSS: No, there's not.

CATHY: There is. It's OK. I'm used to it. I'm just messed up.

RUSS: No, you're not.

CATHY: Thanks for being so nice, Russ.

RUSS: I don't mind. Want to stay here tonight? I mean, you'd have to go in the morning before school or my mom would freak, but I could set the alarm early.

CATHY: No, I don't want to be any trouble.

RUSS: No trouble! Just stay, Cath.

CATHY: No, that's OK.

RUSS: I don't mean anything by it, you know. It would just be us sleeping.

CATHY: I know. But I feel like I've already been enough trouble. Or whatever. Maybe that's the wrong word. But I feel better now. So I'll let you get to sleep. Thanks, Russ.

RUSS: Cathy, don't go like this.

CATHY: *(Smiling.)* Like what? I feel better, Russ. I do. It's helped a lot, talking to you. Being here. I mean it. Thanks.

RUSS: Are you sure?

CATHY: Yeah. Absolutely. You're a great friend.

RUSS: If you're sure . . .

CATHY: Another hug?

(RUSS hugs CATHY again. CATHY climbs out the window and disappears.)

Scene 2: The Light of Day

TY: Did you hear?

RUSS: What?

TY: About Cathy!

RUSS: What about Cathy?

GINA: Did you see Rick? He's a wreck.

RUSS: What's going on?

GINA: It's Cathy.

RUSS: What about her?

MEG: Maybe we shouldn't say. Maybe it's not true. We shouldn't spread rumors.

GINA: They say it's Rick's fault.

MEG: Gina! Don't spread rumors! We don't actually know anything!

RUSS: Was Cathy in an accident or something?

TY: Or something!

RUSS: What?

MEG: I don't know, Russ.

RUSS: Yes, you do.

MEG: We don't know anything for sure. So we shouldn't say anything until we know. If there really is something we need to know, there will be an announcement or something.

RUSS: *(To GINA.)* Did Rick do something to Cathy?

GINA: I don't know. People are saying—

MEG: Gina!

GINA: What!

MEG: Are you deaf? I said we shouldn't say anything until we know for sure.

GINA: You said it, but it doesn't mean I should listen.

MEG: But this is serious. This isn't something silly.

GINA: I know!

MEG: So? Don't you see the difference?

GINA: He's going to hear stuff anyway. Everyone's talking about it. Why shouldn't he hear it from us?

MEG: We shouldn't say anything because we don't know anything for sure. We shouldn't say anything, especially something negative, especially something so serious, if we don't know if it's true. It's wrong. Sometimes I really don't understand people. I mean, something potentially terrible is going on, something really upsetting, and all anybody wants to do is dish about it. I don't understand. How can you be so horrible?

Seriously! This isn't some dumb rumor about Rick kissing Jennifer Holliman or something. This is bigger than that. Have a little respect, Gina. I am seriously so, so disappointed in everyone today. I just can't believe . . . I know I'm up on my soapbox and I'm lecturing and being bossy, but I just feel like I have to! I don't know what else to do. I just think spreading this rumor is so wrong. Please, let's just wait to get the facts!

GINA: You . . . don't get upset at me, Meg. I didn't mean to do anything bad. I just think . . .

MEG: I know! But you see what I'm saying, right?

GINA: I do, but . . . I don't know. It just seems like everyone's talking about it, so there's got to be some truth to it. And like I said, he's going to hear it from someone.

MEG: I know, but . . .

RUSS: You guys are seriously scaring me.

MEG: I'm seriously scared. What if it's true?

RUSS: What if what's true? Can anyone give me a straight answer here?

TY: People are saying—sorry Meg, but I think he needs to know since you've built it up so much—people are saying that Cathy's dead.

RUSS: Dead! What are you talking about?

TY: I don't know the facts, like Meg said, but people are saying she killed herself.

RUSS: Why? You said because of Rick?

GINA: Well, people are saying maybe he cheated on her or something.

MEG: We don't know.

RUSS: But is she really dead?

TY: That part everyone seems to agree on. There have been a whole lot of people, adults, rushing around this morning. Something's up. I heard someone say they're calling a faculty meeting first thing "to figure out how to deal with this."

GINA: So something's happening. It's not a total rumor.

RUSS: How can we know? I want to know!

TY: We could listen in at the teacher's meeting.

MEG: Don't be stupid, Ty.

(RICK enters.)

GINA: Rick!

MEG: Gina, don't. You don't know anything.

GINA: Rick!

(With trepidation, RICK crosses to GINA.)

GINA: What's going on?

RICK: What do you mean?

GINA: I mean, we're hearing a lot of rumors. Do you know what's going on? Is all this stuff true?

RICK: I don't know.

GINA: You don't know?

RICK: I mean, I don't know for sure. I just know what I've heard. I don't know.

GINA: You must know more than that. When did you last see Cathy?

RICK: A couple of nights ago.

GINA: Not yesterday? Or today?

RICK: No. I just . . . I called her house last night. That's all. I don't know any more than you guys. And I certainly didn't do anything to her, if that's what you mean. We broke up anyway, remember? Everyone seems to forget that. I didn't do anything. I was being nice to her. I was going to give her a ride to school since her car isn't working. That's all.

TY: It's OK, man.

GINA: So? What happened when you called?

RICK: I'm not supposed to say.

GINA: We're your friends, Rick.

RICK: You're Cathy's friends.

GINA: And you used to go out with Cathy. So we were—are—your friends, too.

RICK: Yeah, right.

MEG: We're just concerned, Rick. Please. We're getting totally freaked out here. Is she OK?

RICK: Well . . . No.

MEG: Oh my God.

GINA: What do you mean?

RICK: I mean, she's not OK and I'm not supposed to say anything more.

GINA: Well, *someone* must have said something already or the whole school wouldn't be talking about it.

RUSS: Just say it, man.

TY: Come on, Rick. We just want to know.

RICK: Her dad . . . Her dad said for me to call the hospital. He said . . . he said something was wrong. He said . . . There was a lot of noise in the background. Like her mother screaming or crying or something. And her dad, he's always so calm and he was freaked, too. And he said, he said he thought Cathy was dead. I don't even think he knew who he was talking to. He said, "Call an ambulance. My daughter! My daughter!" He just kept saying "my daughter" a lot. And I was like, "What? What?" I couldn't figure out what was going on. Then Mr. Hayes said that—well, maybe I think her mother said, "Cathy's dead! She's dead!" And she was screaming. It was terrible. And her dad's saying, "Call an ambulance!" over and over. So finally, I hung up the phone and I did. Then later I told my parents, and they . . . I don't know what they did. They did something. And they told me later that Cathy killed herself. That she probably killed herself last night.

MEG: Oh my God.

RICK: I know.

GINA: I didn't think . . . I didn't think it could be true.

RICK: I know.

TY: It seems like a joke. It must have seemed like a joke.

RICK: I didn't know what to do. I didn't really think . . . You just don't think it could be . . .

RUSS: But I saw Cathy. Last night. She came to see me. At, like, three A.M.

RICK: That's impossible.

RUSS: Of course it's possible. Just because I wasn't her boyfriend . . .

RICK: No, no. Cathy . . . I called her house at about nine P.M. See? So you didn't see Cathy last night.

MEG: Unless it's not true!

RICK: Meg, I'm sorry to say this. I'm really, really sorry, but her parents . . . This was no joke. This was serious. Even if—But my parents wouldn't tell me Cathy was dead if it wasn't true.

RUSS: But she came to see me. She woke me up!

TY: Maybe it was a dream.

RUSS: No way! It was real. This is all some sick—

RICK: I don't know what or who you saw, but I'm telling you, it wasn't Cathy.

RUSS: But—it seemed so real. I could swear . . .

MEG: None of us can believe this, Russ. It's OK.

RUSS: It seemed so real.

TALK BACK!

1. What do you think was really going on in Scene 1?

2. What do you think about the rumor mill? Do you agree with Meg or Gina?

3. Can you understand or relate to how Cathy felt?

4. Do you think Russ or Rick should have responded differently to Cathy?

5. What do you think about suicide? Is it wrong? Understandable? Is it a chemical imbalance? A character flaw?

THE LITTLE ROOM

2F, 1M

WHO

FEMALES
    Jenny
    Mother

MALES
    Peter

WHERE Scene 1: Jenny's living room, day; Scene 2: Peter's house, night.

WHEN Present day.

To create a genuine sense of horror, you must believe your circumstances, but avoid melodrama or it will turn into a comedy! Also, be sure not to "play the end"; keep the audience guessing until the very end.

This is based on the Bluebeard myth. There are many different variations on this story (see "Talk Back!"). Write a play based on this tale or another folk/fairy tale.

Scene 1: Seduction

MOTHER: I met the nicest boy at the market today.

JENNY: Mom, face it. I don't like the boys you want me to like.

MOTHER: That's why I'm trying to help you. I know better than you do. I have more experience in the world, and I know which boys are going to be nice to you.

JENNY: Can we change the subject? This is sort of gross.

MOTHER: Jenny, he's coming over.

JENNY: What?

MOTHER: This boy.

JENNY: Why?

MOTHER: Because I asked him to. I told him all about you and he wanted to meet you.

JENNY: Mom! I'm not interested.

MOTHER: Jenny, give him a try. He's very nice.

JENNY: Why don't *you* give him a try if you like him so much?

MOTHER: Jenny, don't be smart.

JENNY: Mom, I'm just not interested in anyone my mom sets me up with.

MOTHER: Jenny, he's nice. He goes to York Prep. He drives a brand new BMW. He's polite and charming. He's got everything anyone could want who's got any sense in her head. So just give him a chance, that's all I ask. I really think you might like him if you give him a chance.

JENNY: Mom! I don't—

MOTHER: Jenny, I'm putting my foot down on this. Just give him a chance.

(The doorbell rings.)

MOTHER: That's him. Just fix your hair a little.

JENNY: No. If I have to meet him, then he's going to have to see me as I really am.

MOTHER: *(Sighs.)* Fine. But you might be sorry.

(MOTHER opens the door. PETER enters.)

PETER: Mrs. Hoffman, it's so good to see you again.

MOTHER: Thank you, Peter.

PETER: I bought you these flowers.

MOTHER: Thank you, Peter!

PETER: What a nice house you have.

MOTHER: Thank you so much.

PETER: Did you decorate it yourself?

MOTHER: I did. I'm no decorator, but it turned out OK.

PETER: It turned out great.

MOTHER: Peter, come meet my daughter, Jenny.

PETER: Hello, Jenny.

JENNY: Peter.

MOTHER: Maybe I should leave you two alone so you can get to know one another. I know it can be a little awkward with an adult around. Can I get you anything to drink?

PETER: Oh, sure. How about a Coke?

MOTHER: Sure. Jenny?

JENNY: How about some arsenic?

MOTHER: Always joking. One Coke coming up, Peter.

PETER: Thanks, Mrs. Hoffman.

MOTHER: Why don't you just call me Carol?

PETER: OK, Carol.

(MOTHER exits.)

PETER: Your mother told me a lot about you.

JENNY: I'm sure none of it's true.

PETER: I guess so. She said you were friendly.

JENNY: Nice.

PETER: Jenny, no need to be so . . . Listen, everyone's mother's a drag. Let's just forget about her and have a good time. Want to get out of here and go to my place?

JENNY: I just met you.

PETER: I know. I just thought it might be a nice change of pace for you. My parents are away, as usual, so I have the place to myself. I've got a screening room. We could watch a movie or something, and you could get away from your mother.

JENNY: I don't mind my mother.

PETER: Oh. I thought I sensed some tension.

JENNY: No. That's just how we are. I just don't like it when she brings strangers to the house.

PETER: We're not strangers. You know I'm Peter and I know you're Jenny.

JENNY: I don't know anything about you.

PETER: What's to know? I'm just a regular guy.

JENNY: Right.

PETER: You have really pretty hair.

JENNY: Thanks.

PETER: Do you think your mother would be happy if we got along?

JENNY: Yeah. That's the idea.

PETER: I think it would drive her crazy.

JENNY: I doubt that. Why else do you think you're here?

PETER: But what if we *really* got along? Know what I mean? If you *really* liked me I bet she wouldn't like it at all.

(PETER walks over to JENNY and stands very close to her.)

PETER: You really do have really pretty hair.

(PETER touches JENNY's hair.)

JENNY: Listen, just stop. I don't even know you.

PETER: What? I'm just trying to get to know you. Give a guy a chance.

JENNY: Why should I?

PETER: I felt the same way you did before I came here. I met your mother and she was a very pleasant woman. I liked her. And to be honest, I was bored. I live alone in a big house. It's winter break at school, so all my classmates are off with their families. So I'm bored. Really bored. When your mom and I started talking, at first it was just something to do. She invited me over. I thought, "Why not? You've got nothing else going on." Then she mentioned you. I saw the setup a mile away. I wasn't crazy about it. All mothers brag about their kids. I thought I was going to come in to see Quasimodo. Instead, I got you. And I'm pleasantly surprised. Your mother didn't do you justice. And she bragged like all mothers do. Well, most. I don't even know if my mother remembers my name. But there's something about you, Jenny. I like you. You're . . . I don't want to embarrass you, but you're the prettiest girl I think I've ever seen.

JENNY: Please.

PETER: I mean it. Believe me. It's embarrassing to say it, but I feel like I have to. I don't know if we're meant to be or anything, we did just meet, but I like you. Instinctively.

JENNY: If I'm the prettiest girl you've ever seen, then you need to get out more.

PETER: *(Laughs.)* Maybe so. But I doubt it. You're clever, too. I like that. Jenny, don't you like me at all?

JENNY: I don't know. It's hard to say.

PETER: I'm not completely awful?

JENNY: No. Not so far.

PETER: And I've been nice?

JENNY: Well, yeah.

PETER: So? Why not give it a try? What do you have to lose? Worst-case scenario, you get a lot of compliments and see a movie.

JENNY: I guess.

PETER: Come on, Jenny. It would bug your mom, too, if we left. Come over to my place. It'll be a good time. I promise.

(MOTHER enters with PETER's Coke.)

MOTHER: Here you go, Peter.

PETER: Sorry, Mrs. Hoffman. I've got to go home. Jenny's coming with me.

MOTHER: What?

PETER: At least I think so. Jenny?

JENNY: Maybe.

PETER: Tell you what. I'll wait at my BMW while you decide.

(PETER exits.)

MOTHER: Are you going?

JENNY: Do you want me to go?

MOTHER: I don't know. I'd rather you stay here.

JENNY: Then maybe I'll go.

MOTHER: He is a nice boy, though.

JENNY: Or maybe not.

MOTHER: Go, Jenny.

JENNY: Mom, can't I make my own decision? You always boss me around and push me into things. I'm nearly an adult. I want to make my own choices. You can't decide for me forever, you know. I have to start doing things on my own sometime. And I don't know what I think of this guy. I just met him. What makes you so sure all the time that your judgment is right? I think he might be a player. I think he probably comes on to girls all the time. He's not just a good boy who goes to the prep school. And just because he's got money doesn't mean he's nice or better than us. I think you actually think that, Mom. It's sick. Just because someone's got a BMW and has decent manners doesn't mean they're nice. But I do envy him a little. He has a whole house to himself with no mother to tell him what to do.

MOTHER: Jenny, be nice.

JENNY: You can't tell me what to do.

MOTHER: Yes, I can.

JENNY: That's it. I'm leaving. Anything to get out of this house and away from your tyranny!

(JENNY storms out of the house and slams the door.)

MOTHER: Good. That's what I wanted anyway.

Scene 2: Behind the Door

PETER: So, here we are.

JENNY: Yup.

PETER: Why don't you make yourself comfortable.

JENNY: I'm pretty comfortable.

PETER: Great. Want a drink?

JENNY: Sure.

PETER: I can get some wine from the wine cellar.

JENNY: OK.

PETER: God, you look gorgeous, Jenny.

JENNY: Thanks.

PETER: I mean it. Don't be embarrassed. I just had to say it. *(Beat.)* Tell you what. You pick a movie, and I'll go get that wine. Make yourself at home. Just don't go into that little room on the left. Otherwise, what's mine is yours. You can go anywhere else you like. Feel free to check out the upstairs if you want. Be back soon.

JENNY: OK.

(PETER exits. JENNY looks around the room for a moment, then finds herself drawn to the room off stage left. She tries to look through the crack in the door, but doesn't see anything. She tentatively

touches the door handle and finds the room is un-locked. She walks away for a moment. Filled with curiosity, she checks that PETER is not coming back, then she returns to the door. Carefully, she turns the doorknob and opens the door. JENNY enters the room. We hear her gasp after a beat and she runs out of the room and shuts the door quickly.)

JENNY: Oh my God. Oh my God!

(PETER reenters.)

PETER: OK, I got a nice vintage—Jenny, what's wrong? You look odd.

JENNY: Nothing! Nothing.

PETER: Nothing.

JENNY: Nothing at all. I just . . . thought I saw a mouse.

(PETER puts the wine bottle on a table.)

PETER: Is that how you got blood on your shoes?

JENNY: What?

PETER: There's blood on your shoes. You went into the little room.

JENNY: I didn't.

PETER: You did. You just couldn't listen, could you? Well, know what? Neither could she. No one stays. No one listens. Everyone lies and disobeys.

That's why I had to do that to her. And the others. No one can just do the one thing I ask of them! It's unbelievable! Women—you're all dirty. I would have given you anything, Jenny. Anything you wanted. Look around! I've got loads of money. You could be wealthy and have a guy who's crazy about you. I really do think you're pretty. I would have been good to you. But you had to go and do the one thing—I am so disappointed. I thought you were different. So clever, and yet so stupid. Everyone lets me down. So now I have to do the same thing to you I did to the others. I didn't want to, Jenny. I didn't. It's not as if I enjoy it. Well, truth be told, I do enjoy it a little. That's why I take my time. You just couldn't be good, Jenny.

JENNY: I'm sorry, Peter.

PETER: Of course you are. Because you're going to die. They're all sorry later.

JENNY: The thing is, Peter, I like you, too.

PETER: Right. So what was all that protesting?

JENNY: I just hate to do anything my mother wants me to do. But you had a point before. I think we should do something my mother wouldn't like.

PETER: Really?

JENNY: Really.

PETER: You're still going to die.

JENNY: Listen, Peter, I just wanted to know more about you.

PETER: So now you know more about me.

JENNY: And I still want to make my mother angry. And . . . well . . . you are pretty cute.

PETER: You're a good girl, Jenny. I'm still going to kill you, but maybe I'll be quicker.

JENNY: Take off your jacket.

(PETER takes off his jacket, smiling.)

JENNY: Could you put on some music?

PETER: Of course.

(PETER turns away and JENNY grabs the wine bottle and hits him with it, knocking him out. JENNY stands for a beat looking at PETER's body. She goes back to the little room on the left. JENNY takes a deep breath and reenters the room. She emerges a moment later with an ax.)

JENNY: You've killed your last girl, Peter. I wonder if the others saw through you like I did? Or maybe they truly liked you. Who knows why? Does your mother know what a monster you are? Maybe you killed her, too. Or maybe she never comes home because she can see what you are. Just so you know, my mother has never chosen my boyfriends, and she is never, never, never going to choose one now. In fact, if she so much as suggests a boy is nice, I won't even go near him. You are sick, Peter. I don't want to kill you, though. I don't want to kill anyone. I'm not like you. But what choice do I have? Kill or be killed. And I don't want to die. I don't want anyone else to die either, especially like that girl—how could anyone do that? You are one sick puppy, Peter. (*JENNY takes a deep breath.*) Say your prayers.

TALK BACK!

1. The Bluebeard myth has variations in many cultures and throughout history. In some, the male is made out to be a monster or a stranger/foreigner. Why do you think that is the case?

2. In some versions, the females are put in a negative light: the mother is portrayed as greedy; the daughter is overly curious and, therefore, deserves the male's wrath. What do you think of this?

3. What makes Jenny accept Peter's advances?

4. What do you think is the moral of this tale? What would the moral be if Peter was victorious in the end?

5. Who is to blame in this story: The mother for pushing Jenny to go out with Peter? Jenny for her curiosity? Peter for being a serial killer?

6. Does the mother have Jenny's best interests at heart?

SIGNS

8F, 1M

WHO

FEMALES   MALES
  Alyssa   Shea
  Fawn
  Fergie
  Peyton
  Shelley
  Ivy
  Shahira

WHERE Outside school.

WHEN After school. The scenes are three days apart.

Here's a rehearsal idea: Try having Ivy literally on Shea's back during their discussion in Scene 1. See if you can think of other ways to physicalize what's going on behind the words. Be sure to check in and see how you feel about all this pushing and pulling. Is it exciting? Irritating? Does it make you feel weak? Powerful? Of course, you want to do the exercise fully without actually harming any other actors in the process!

Use the idea of a street sign to construct your own play, using these characters or others. Here are some ideas: Falling Rocks, Deer Crossing, Slow, and Construction Ahead. Some foreign countries also have very interesting signs; for example, England has Humped Zebra Crossing and Changed Priorities Ahead. Feel free to research for more unusual titles.

33

Scene 1: Stop

SHEA: Ivy . . .

IVY: Yes?

SHEA: I think we should see other people.

IVY: What?

SHEA: I don't think we should see each other any more.

IVY: Why? I thought things were going well. I went to your swim meet yesterday.

SHEA: Yeah, well, I just think that we don't have a lot in common.

IVY: Sure we do.

SHEA: No, we don't.

IVY: What do you mean?

SHEA: I'm just not ready for something serious.

IVY: It doesn't have to be serious. We've young, right?

SHEA: Well, right. That's what I mean.

IVY: And I agree with you. So we're OK, right?

SHEA: No. Ivy, I want to see other people.

IVY: Like who?

SHEA: I don't know. Other people.

IVY: If you don't know who . . . I'm not good enough for you?

SHEA: It's not that. We're just too different, you know?

IVY: No, I don't know.

SHEA: Well, that's just how it is.

IVY: Why? Why are you being such a jerk to me?

SHEA: I'm not . . . I'm trying to be nice about it, but you won't let it go.

IVY: What did I do wrong?

SHEA: You didn't do anything wrong. I'm just not looking for this. I don't want this.

IVY: What's "this"?

SHEA: What?

IVY: What's the "this" that you don't want?

SHEA: This hassle.

IVY: This hassle. Would you think it was a hassle if I was prettier?

SHEA: Yes.

IVY: So I'm a hassle to be around.

SHEA: You're too serious. You want too much. You want to be around me all the time. I'm not interested in that. I'm sure there's some other guy who is. But I'm not that guy. I want to play the field, have fun. I don't want to be serious and committed and in a relationship at my age. That's just not who I am. That's who you are, though. So I can't be who you want me to be any more than you can be what I want. We're different. It's nothing personal. It's just how it is. So you should just find a guy who's into all that stuff.

IVY: You're that guy.

SHEA: I'm not that guy.

IVY: You could be.

SHEA: I couldn't be. Don't you get it? I don't want it. I'm not interested in it. *I'm not interested in you.* I didn't want to say it like that, but you leave me no choice. You're not my type. I thought maybe you were, but now that I know you better, I know you're not. So just let it alone. Don't make me say any more because I might say something we both regret. But I'm done with all this. We're over, Ivy.

IVY: I don't understand you. I don't understand where all of this is coming from. How could you do this to me? How could you say—Why are you being so mean? Why did you go out with me in the first place if you hate me so much?

SHEA: I don't hate you.

IVY: If you like me, why are you breaking up with me now?

SHEA: I don't like you that way, Ivy. I though maybe I did, but I don't.

IVY: Don't say, "We could be friends."

SHEA: I wasn't going to.

IVY: You're horrible, Shea, and I hate you. I never want to see you again.

SHEA: Fine. See ya, Ivy. Have a nice life.

IVY: Have a horrible life, Shea.

(SHEA exits.)

IVY: Oh my God, he did *not* just do that! Ohmygod ohmygod ohmygod. What am I going to do? I can't believe—

(FERGIE enters.)

FERGIE: You OK?

IVY: No. I'm not OK. Not at all.

FERGIE: What's wrong?

IVY: My boyfriend just broke up with me!

FERGIE: Oh my God, that's the worst.

IVY: Has this ever happened to you?

FERGIE: No, but I know it's bad.

IVY: I feel like I'm going to die. And I just don't understand. We were getting along so well. And I was going to his swim meets and doing everything he wanted to do—Why couldn't he like me? Why didn't he like me more? I don't know what else I could have done. I really don't.

FERGIE: Well that's just it. You were doing everything for him, so now he thinks he's hot.

IVY: So? That's sort of how I wanted him to feel.

FERGIE: But now he feels like he's so hot that he can get a girl who was out of his league before. He thinks he can be a player now.

IVY: No. Shea is nice. He's not like that. That's why I liked him.

FERGIE: Shea Curtis?

IVY: Yeah.

FERGIE: I'm sorry to tell you this, but he's into Alyssa Jones. I'm only saying this for your own good. The sooner you know what a dog he is, the sooner you'll get over him.

IVY: Alyssa Jones? She's not his type.

FERGIE: Looks like she is. She's not really interested, I don't think, but he is all over her every chance he gets.

IVY: When? How long has this been going on?

FERGIE: For about, I don't know, two weeks now.

IVY: How do you know?

FERGIE: I saw him. I have history with Shea and Alyssa and he's all over her nonstop. If it makes you feel any better, I think she just finds him irritating.

IVY: Two weeks? But we've only been going out for three.

FERGIE: You've been seeing this guy for three weeks, and you're already planning out your life with him? That is sad.

IVY: You don't understand. Everything was going perfectly. We had a connection. We *have* a connection; only he doesn't know it.

FERGIE: Mmm-hmm. I see. Let me guess. You've been letting him get his way about *everything*, haven't you?

IVY: That is not your business.

FERGIE: I'm only trying to help.

IVY: Well, it's none of your business.

FERGIE: Have it your way. But I know I'm right.

IVY: How do you know?

FERGIE: Why else would you be all caught up about him after only three weeks?

IVY: So what if it was like that? That's normal.

FERGIE: I'm just saying, that's how it goes. That's why you're so upset.

IVY: So?

FERGIE: So nothing. I'm just stating the facts. Best thing for you to do is find another guy.

IVY: Like revenge?

FERGIE: No, someone you like better.

IVY: If he saw me with another guy, I bet he'd freak.

FERGIE: You are too desperate.

IVY: What?

FERGIE: That's why he broke up with you. That's why this is going to keep happening to you.

IVY: What do you know about it?

FERGIE: I know a lot about it.

IVY: You said no one broke up with you.

FERGIE: I have eyes. I see how it goes. And I broke up with a guy for the same reason Shea broke up with you. You want too much. You're too clingy. You need to take it easy. You shouldn't let the other person think they're powerful. You should never let a guy have all the control. That's a one-way route to being treated like a dishrag. And this is how I know. With this guy I was with, it was fun for a little while to boss him around. It really was. Anything I'd say, he'd do. He never had his own opinions. I got to pick what movies we'd see, what food we'd eat, where we'd go and when. I could be really mean to him, say whatever I wanted, and he just bounced back. Like a puppy dog, he just showed up for more kicking. But then it got boring. I got so sick of him never having anything to say for himself. Having to always be in charge. I wanted a *man*, you know? Someone who could stand up for himself. It just stopped being fun and starting being sad and boring. And that's what you are now, sad and boring.

IVY: But I have opinions. And my opinion is that we should stay together. I'm not like that guy at all.

FERGIE: You said yourself that you'd do what he wanted to do. What did he ever do for you?

IVY: Lots of things.

FERGIE: Face facts. He doesn't want you. And the more you want him, the more he'll want to run away. Try playing it cool next time. Pretend like you don't care.

IVY: I guess you think you're an expert.

FERGIE: I just know that when someone holds on too tight, it feels like you're choking.

IVY: How poetic.

FERGIE: It's true.

IVY: *(Sarcastic.)* Well, thanks for your great advice.

FERGIE: Just trying to help. Really. Don't feel bad. You can do better than him.

(FERGIE exits.)

IVY: No, I can't. And I don't want to.

Scene 2: Yield

IVY: Hey, Alyssa? Can I talk to you?

ALYSSA: If it's quick. I have things to do.

IVY: It'll be quick. I just wanted to help you out.

ALYSSA: How?

IVY: Well, I just broke up with Shea Curtis, and I hear he's bugging you now.

ALYSSA: He said he broke up with you.

IVY: That's just it. He's a liar. I thought you should know.

ALYSSA: Uh-huh. So you're just being helpful.

IVY: Right.

ALYSSA: He says you're hanging on him like a leech.

IVY: Exactly my point. Do you see me hanging on him now?

ALYSSA: I guess not. But maybe this is some kind of a game.

IVY: What kind of a game?

ALYSSA: How should I know? Anyway, I'm not interested in Shea anyway. I've got a boyfriend.

IVY: Oh good. He's a lousy kisser, anyhow.

ALYSSA: You sound jealous.

IVY: Jealous of what?

ALYSSA: Him liking me.

IVY: You can have him.

ALYSSA: Well, I don't want him. You should talk to Peyton.

IVY: Why?

ALYSSA: Shea's been hitting on her, too, and I think she might like him back. So you'd better hurry if you want to stop him from seeing her.

IVY: That's not what I'm trying to do.

ALYSSA: Right. Been there, done that.

(ALYSSA exits. FAWN enters.)

FAWN: Did it work?

IVY: She says she doesn't want him anyway. But that he's also hitting on Peyton, and she might want to go out with him, too!

FAWN: I hate to say it, Ivy, but maybe Shea is really a dog.

IVY: But he's my dog! I know it's nuts, Fawn, but I think we should be together.

FAWN: You're such a romantic.

IVY: Am I? I think I'm being realistic. Am I just nuts? If we're meant to be together, why can't he see it?

FAWN: He's a guy. And he's young. They're stupid. We have to help them see what they're missing.

IVY: When should you fight for what you want and when should you give up?

FAWN: If you give up, you're a quitter.

IVY: But are there ever times you should give up?

FAWN: I don't think so.

IVY: What if maybe you shouldn't want what you want? What if what you want is bad for you?

FAWN: So now you think Shea is bad for you? I'm just going by what you've told me, and you say that you two are perfect together. If that's true, he just needs help seeing it.

(SHEA enters with PEYTON.)

IVY: I don't know . . .

FAWN: There you-know-who is with you-know-who!

(IVY turns around and sees SHEA and PEYTON.)

FAWN: Don't turn around!

IVY: Too late! Great. Now he's seen me turning around. Why is he with her?

FAWN: They look very chummy.

IVY: Did I tell you Alyssa said that Shea said that he broke up with me?

FAWN: Well, he did.

IVY: But he's not supposed to say so. And she said that he said that I was leeching onto him.

FAWN: As if! You're over here and he's over there. I'd hardly call that leeching. Oh my God, don't look.

(IVY turns around and sees SHEA kiss PEYTON. SHEA exits.)

IVY: I hate him. He did that to make me jealous.

FAWN: That just shows that he still cares about you. Go talk to Peyton now! I'll catch up with you later.

IVY: I have to destroy him, Fawn. I want to make him untouchable to anyone else.

FAWN: Do it.

(FAWN exits.)

IVY: Hi!

PEYTON: Hi!

IVY: I see you're . . . with Shea.

PEYTON: Uh-huh.

IVY: I used to go out with him.

PEYTON: Who are you again?

IVY: Ivy.

PEYTON: Oooooo. Ivy.

IVY: What does that mean?

PEYTON: He told me about you.

IVY: He's so immature. Alyssa said he was spreading lies about me.

PEYTON: Well, it seems like he was telling the truth.

IVY: He wouldn't know the truth if it walked into him.

PEYTON: He said you were trying to scare off other girls so you could have him for yourself.

IVY: I don't want him. He was lousy, if you get what I mean.

PEYTON: Right.

IVY: But maybe you have lower standards.

PEYTON: You're just jealous. It's pathetic. I happen to know that Shea is a fantastic guy, if you get what I mean.

IVY: You're disgusting and desperate.

PEYTON: I'm desperate? You wrote the book on it.

IVY: You are going to regret saying that.

PEYTON: I don't think so.

(SHEA *walks in, flirting with SHELLEY and* SHAHIRA.)

SHELLEY: Stop, Shea, you are so bad!

SHAHIRA: You should come over to my house later. My mom's going to be working a late shift.

SHELLEY: I thought we were going out for burgers!

SHEA: Girls! Girls! There's enough of me to go around.

PEYTON: I don't think so. I know what you've got to give and there's definitely not enough to go around.

(PEYTON *exits.*)

SHEA: Peyton? What's up with you?

SHAHIRA: What is she talking about?

SHEA: I don't know. She's just into me. I can't help that.

IVY: What's wrong with you?

SHEA: Oh great. Here we go.

IVY: No. It's not what you think. I see you clearly now. You're a pig.

SHEA: Ladies, do not listen to this woman. She is psycho.

IVY: No, I'm not. You are.

SHEA: Right. You're the one begging to have me back.

IVY: No, I'm not. I just want to know what's wrong with you.

SHEA: There's nothing wrong with me.

IVY: Why do you chase after anything with legs?

SHEA: I'm not chasing after you. Not just any legs will do.

IVY: You're sick.

SHEA: How many times do I have to tell you, woman? I am a guy. A young guy. I don't want to be married. I don't want to be in love. I want to have a good time. That's what people do when they're young. There's nothing wrong with that. I have the whole rest of my life to be serious if I want. I am not going to waste my time doing that now. And if I can have a good time with some girls, some good-looking, hot girls, that's what I'm going to do. It's human nature. Men want to get around. It's in all the history books.

IVY: That's not what you said to me.

SHEA: I've said that to you, like, fifty times!

IVY: Not at first! At first you said you said—

SHEA: Who cares what I said before? Listen to what I'm saying now. Now I'm saying that I'm a young guy and I'm going to party. If I can go out with a lot of girls, I am going to do that! I'd be crazy not to! Don't tell me that if a bunch of guys wanted you, you wouldn't be really into it.

IVY: I wouldn't be! I'd pick the one I liked best.

SHAHIRA: So would I.

SHELLEY: Not me. If I had two hot guys into me, I'd juggle them for sure!

SHEA: If you say you wouldn't love it, you're lying. Why have just one person giving you attention and compliments if you could have many? It just doesn't make sense.

IVY: I didn't say I wouldn't love it, but I wouldn't play people like that. It's not fair. Don't you care that you're hurting people's feelings?

SHEA: I can't help it if people take themselves too seriously. That's not my problem.

IVY: I don't understand you at all. Why did I ever like you? You've changed.

SHEA: Maybe I have. I think it's for the better. Let's go, ladies.

SHAHIRA: I'm going. But not with you. I deserve a man who respects me.

SHEA: Good luck.

SHAHIRA: Good riddance.

(IVY and SHAHIRA exit.)

SHEA: Am I going nuts? Because I think I make sense.

SHELLEY: I think so, too. Why have one guy if you can have two?

SHEA: Do you have another guy?

SHELLEY: Of course I do! I'm too young to get serious about anybody. I'm going to play the field until I'm ready to get married. If I *ever* get married. Who knows? I want a career. I'm going to be a journalist. I don't know too many guys who want to go to war zones for the fun of it. And who wants kids? Kids just scream and poop and complain. Besides, why should guys have all the fun? I know guys are going to run around anyway—what's the point of sitting around waiting for a call? I'm just gonna call someone else, then. Play or be played. That's what I say. And as long as I'm in control of things, I'm happy. You won't see me waiting for a call on Friday night. No way. I'm out. Catch me if you can.

SHEA: You're seeing someone else?

SHELLEY: I'm seeing two other guys.

SHEA: We're over, baby.

SHELLEY: What's your problem?

SHEA: You're dirty.

SHELLEY: You don't know what I do or don't do.

SHEA: Still!

SHELLEY: So it's OK for you to play around but not me?

SHEA: That's right.

SHELLEY: See ya.

(SHELLEY starts to leave.)

SHEA: Wait! So that's it?

SHELLEY: What? We're done.

SHEA: You're not going to cry?

SHELLEY: As if.

(SHELLEY exits.)

SHEA: I do not understand women.

TALK BACK!

1. Was Ivy too possessive or did Shea turn into a jerk?

2. Who has more self-confidence and self-respect, Shahira or Shelley?

3. Are relationships basically a power struggle? Can they ever be even-sided?

4. Do you agree with Shea's point of view about dating? Why or why not?

5. If you care a lot about someone, should you pretend to be indifferent so you don't seem desperate? Is that dishonest or self-preservation?

6. When should you fight for a relationship and when should you give up?

7. How do you know when someone's not right for you? How do you know when a relationship is over?

8. What's the best way to break up with someone? What's the best way to get over a breakup?

MINE

2F, 3M

WHO

FEMALES	MALES
Emily	Jay
Gina	Sim
	Troy

WHERE Outside school.

WHEN After school. The scenes are one day apart.

Each character must decide when he or she is telling the truth and when he or she is lying. If you lie, why? Know your reasons. Be very clear about why you say what you say at all times.

Write a scene that sets up Sim and Gina's previous relationship. Then write a scene that takes place after this play ends. What happens? What's the aftermath?

Scene 1: Up Against a Wall

GINA: So what are we doing tonight?

TROY: Any ideas?

GINA: No.

TROY: We could see a movie.

   (SIM enters.)

GINA: None I want to see.

TROY: We could see *Storm Legion.*

GINA: Saw it.

TROY: How was it?

GINA: Dunno.

TROY: You don't know.

GINA: OK, I guess.

TROY: We could do nothing, then.

GINA: OK.

   (GINA sees SIM.)

GINA: Oh God.

TROY: What?

GINA: Nothing.

TROY: Him?

GINA: No. Nothing.

TROY: OK.

GINA: Let's go somewhere.

TROY: I thought you didn't want to do anything.

GINA: Changed my mind. Let's just go somewhere else.

SIM: I can hear you.

TROY: What?

SIM: I can hear you.

TROY: I didn't think you were deaf. But we weren't talking to you.

SIM: Whatever.

GINA: Let's go, Troy.

TROY: Is it this guy?

GINA: Well, yeah.

TROY: Is he bothering you?

GINA: Sort of.

TROY: What's the deal?

GINA: No deal.

SIM: I don't even want to talk to you, Gina. So get over
yourself.

GINA: Get lost, Sim.

TROY: You heard her. Clear off.

SIM: I don't have to.

TROY: I think you do.

SIM: It's a free country.

TROY: Not anymore it's not. Clear off.

SIM: I have as much right to stand here as you.

GINA: Don't worry about it, Troy. Let's just go.

TROY: How come this guy bothers you? Did he do
something I should know about?

GINA: No. I hardly know him.

SIM: That's not true.

GINA: Yes, it is.

SIM: You're ashamed of me.

GINA: I don't know what you're talking about. Leave
me alone.

TROY: I am losing my patience with you. Leave her alone, OK?

SIM: She used to be my girlfriend.

GINA: No, I wasn't.

SIM: Yes, you were. She saw *Storm Legion* with me. We made out the whole time.

GINA: As if! Don't be disgusting. As if I'd kiss you.

SIM: You did.

GINA: Troy, let's get out of here.

SIM: We went out for two months. You introduced me to your parents. We went to the circus. I took you out to a fancy restaurant one time. You like Italian food. Your favorite color is red. You like action movies. You like old rock music from the sixties. You recycle—and all the time, not just every once in a while like other people. You actually clean out cans and stuff before you throw them away. You like dolphins. You want a tattoo of one on your ankle, but your dad won't let you get it. I know everything about you, Gina. We were close. And you know it. And you didn't even tell me . . . I didn't know until I saw you . . . What are you doing with this guy? I thought you hated people like this. Why couldn't you even tell me? Why can't you admit—Are you ashamed of me or something? Are you just too cool for me now?

GINA: I don't know what he's talking about.

SIM: I was your first boyfriend, Gina.

GINA: Shut up! You don't know what you're talking about, creep. I don't know what your problem is with me. Stop stalking me. I don't know you. We never went out. Like I'd go to the circus? I definitely never introduced you to my family. I don't know you. So you can leave me alone now. Find another girl to fixate on, please! I don't mean to be mean, but I just don't know you. So you need to stop stalking me. I don't know how you know things about me, but it's really creeping me out. So if you're going through my trash or sitting outside my bedroom window—

SIM: You told me those things!

GINA: *I don't know you.* Please, just leave me alone! What do I need to do to get you to leave me alone?

TROY: He wants you to do him.

SIM: That's not what I want!

GINA: Well, there's no way that's happening! I don't like you. I have not and will not kiss you or do anything else with you. So, if that's what you have in mind, you can forget it. I'm not your girlfriend and I never will be. Stop stalking me. It's scaring me.

SIM: I am not stalking you!

GINA: You show up everywhere. You're creeping me out!

SIM: Gina, you like me. You went out with me. I don't know why you're being like—

TROY: OK, loser. Get lost before I tear your face off.

SIM: This is none of your business.

TROY: I think it is.

SIM: I think it's not. I'm just talking to Gina. This has nothing to do with you.

TROY: Get lost now, buddy.

SIM: Gina, I don't get why you're acting like this. What's your problem?

GINA: You're my problem. I don't even know you. I was nice to you once and now you're like a psycho.

SIM: But—we were something . . . I mean we had—

TROY: I've had enough. You need to shut up and leave her alone now. I mean it.

SIM: I think you should get lost. Gina is my girlfriend. She's just trying to make me jealous or something.

GINA: Troy, I don't know what he's talking about.

SIM: She told me she loved me.

GINA: No, I didn't!

SIM: I bought her a bracelet for Valentine's Day.

GINA: I didn't want it!

SIM: You said you loved it!

GINA: Shut up!

SIM: Not until you admit—

(*TROY pushes SIM against the wall.*)

TROY: You need to leave now.

SIM: You can't bully me into doing what you want.

TROY: Do you want to find out?

SIM: Get your hands off of me.

GINA: He's not worth it, Troy. Let's just get out of here.

TROY: I think this psycho should get out of here.

GINA: I don't want to be here anyway.

(*JAY enters.*)

JAY: What's going on, Troy?

TROY: This little turd thinks he can take me, Jay.

JAY: What are you on, little turd? You don't want to
    start anything with Troy here. He'll cream a little
    turd like you.

SIM: You don't scare me.

JAY: Oh no?

SIM: No.

JAY: You look scared. Doesn't the little turd look scared, Troy?

TROY: This is one scared little turd. And I think you should apologize, little turd, to Gina.

SIM: For what? For talking?

JAY: You are asking for it, turd.

TROY: Say you're sorry.

GINA: Let's just get out of here, Troy. He's nothing. Let's just go do something.

SIM: I am something!

JAY: Right. You're a turd. Maybe we should put the turd in the toilet, Troy.

TROY: There's an idea. We should flush this turd.

GINA: Let's go, Troy.

TROY: He was giving you a hard time, Gina. That is not acceptable. No turd is going to give you a hard time.

SIM: Gina, please. You know this isn't right. This isn't you.

TROY: Don't talk to her with your turd mouth. You never kissed that turd mouth did you, Gina?

GINA: No. But maybe you should just let him go. He's learned his lesson.

JAY: I don't think so.

TROY: Neither do I. I think it's time we flush this turd.

(JAY and Troy start to drag SIM offstage.)

GINA: Guys, don't! He's not worth it!

SIM: See? You care about me, Gina. I knew it!

JAY: Gina? Did you used to go out with this turd?

GINA: No?

TROY: Do you want me to stop? Do you want to save this pathetic little piece of crap?

GINA: No.

TROY: Say it to him, Gina.

GINA: You need to leave me alone.

TROY: Call him a little turd.

GINA: Troy!

TROY: Gina, do you want him to leave you alone or not?

GINA: Leave me alone, little turd.

SIM: Gina—

GINA: Get him away from me. Please.

JAY: You heard the lady, turd. You're coming with us.

TROY: Don't worry, Gina, he won't bother you again.

JAY: He won't bother anyone again when we're done.

SIM: Gina, tell them to stop! You don't want this to happen. I know you don't.

(Beat. GINA says nothing. TROY and JAY drag SIM offstage.)

Scene 2: Standing Up

EMILY: Gina, what do you want to do tonight?

GINA: Dunno.

EMILY: We could see a movie.

GINA: Which one?

JAY: We can hang in my basement.

EMILY: I'm sick of doing that.

JAY: That's not what you said yesterday.

EMILY: That was yesterday. This is today.

TROY: I'm hungry.

GINA: Pizza?

EMILY: What else? Who's got money?

(SIM enters.)

TROY: I'm broke.

GINA: Troy, you're supposed to pay for me.

TROY: You wish!

EMILY: Very gentlemanly.

TROY: Did I ever say I was a gentleman?

JAY: If you said it, you'd be lying.

(GINA sees SIM.)

GINA: Let's go.

(TROY sees SIM.)

TROY: Well, well, well. Who do we have here?

JAY: I believe it is the little turd.

TROY: Didn't we get rid of you yet?

JAY: I think he's back for more, Troy.

TROY: Impossible. I thought we made ourselves clear. Is he still bothering you, Gina?

GINA: Not yet. Not so far. Why don't you go, Sim? It's for the best.

(SIM doesn't speak.)

JAY: What's the matter, kid? Cat got your tongue?

(SIM doesn't answer.)

TROY: Get lost, kid. While you still can.

(SIM stands still.)

EMILY: What's wrong with him?

JAY: This is the kid we taught a lesson to last week.

EMILY: What do you mean "taught a lesson to"?

JAY: We kicked the crap out of him. Didn't we?

(JAY pushes SIM. SIM doesn't react other than regaining his balance.)

EMILY: Jay! You shouldn't beat people up. You'll get in trouble.

JAY: No, I won't.

TROY: No one cares about trash like him.

EMILY: He's standing right there!

JAY: Duh.

EMILY: Gina, back me up here.

(GINA doesn't say anything.)

EMILY: *(To SIM.)* What do you want, anyway?

GINA: He wants me.

EMILY: You?

GINA: He thinks we used to go out.

EMILY: Did you?

GINA: No.

SIM: Yes.

GINA: No, Sim. Just go away now.

(GINA turns her back on SIM.)

EMILY: Listen, Sim, right? Gina doesn't seem to like you, and I'm sure you don't want to get beat up. So maybe you should go now. For your own sake.

(SIM doesn't respond. He stares at GINA's back.)

EMILY: Seriously. I don't think these guys are joking.

JAY: It's a lost cause, Emily. I think he's a retard.

GINA: Can we go now, Troy?

TROY: Do you want me to take care of this guy again? 'Cause I'd be happy to.

GINA: No. Let's go.

TROY: 'K. Let's go, guys. Don't follow us, retard.

SIM: Nobody's going anywhere.

JAY: Says who?

SIM: Says me.

(SIM pulls out a gun.)

EMILY: **Oh my God**!

JAY: Is that real?

SIM: It's real.

TROY: I bet it's not.

EMILY: Shut up, Troy! *(Beat.)* Listen, Sim? I don't know what's going on here, but . . . please. There's got to be a way we can work this out. Please! I—I don't want to die. You're not really going to shoot anyone are you?

SIM: I don't know.

EMILY: Don't. Please. Think of yourself. Do you want to spend your life in jail?

SIM: I don't care.

EMILY: You do care. You must care! You've got your whole life ahead of you. Don't let anybody take that away from you. *(Beat.)* Honestly, these guys don't mean anything by it. They're just jerks sometimes. I'm sure they'll leave you alone if you want. Right, guys?

JAY: Sure.

TROY: Yeah, yeah. Whatever you want.

EMILY: See? They'll leave you alone now. Look, we're all just kids here. We all have done stupid things. I don't know anything about you, but I know I've done some really dumb things. And I've been really depressed, too. But—you can fix it. It will get better. If you let it! Please, please, please, just don't . . . Just don't. You'll regret it. Please. This isn't the answer. I'm sure you don't really want to kill anyone. You just want to be left alone, right?

SIM: I think I do want to kill someone.

EMILY: Sim, please, you'll be ruining your life, too. Think about this for a minute. Just don't.

SIM: I don't care about my life. My life is pathetic. Isn't it?

EMILY: No, Sim—

SIM: *(Pointing the gun at EMILY.)* Shut up! I don't want to hear anything more from you. Shut up. I want to hear from Troy.

(Beat as SIM points the gun at TROY.)

SIM: Am I pathetic?

TROY: No.

SIM: Am I a little turd?

TROY: No.

SIM: Are you sorry you beat me up?

TROY: N—Yes, yes! I'm sorry.

SIM: You're lying.

TROY: No, I mean it. It was wrong.

SIM: *(Pointing the gun at JAY.)* How about you? You seemed to enjoy yourself.

JAY: No. I . . .

SIM: Not so brave now, are you?

(*JAY doesn't speak.*)

SIM: Are you?

JAY: No.

SIM: Are you a retard?

JAY: Well, no.

SIM: Yes, you are. Say it!

JAY: Yes, I am.

SIM: The whole thing.

JAY: I'm a retard.

SIM: And a big turd.

JAY: And a big turd.

EMILY: (*Quietly.*) Sim?

SIM: I'm not talking to you!

EMILY: Sorry! I'm sorry.

SIM: Just shut up. This isn't about you. This is about
Gina. (*Beat.*) Why are you telling lies?

GINA: I'm . . . I don't understand what you want
from me.

SIM: I want you to admit you went out with me.

GINA: We went out once.

SIM: Not once! Many times.

GINA: But—I meant . . . we went out once upon a time. In the past.

SIM: Not so far in the past.

GINA: I guess not.

SIM: And you liked me.

   (Beat.)

GINA: I guess.

SIM: You did!

GINA: I thought I did.

SIM: You did! Why are you lying!

GINA: Sim, it's just that . . . Sim, can you put that gun away? You're scaring me.

SIM: No.

GINA: Please? For me?

SIM: What did you ever do for me? I did everything for you, Gina. I bought you things; I took you places. I was so good to you. This guy doesn't do anything for you. Why . . . I don't understand why you would do this. Any of this. I don't understand. Tell me why.

GINA: I don't know what to tell you.

SIM: Yes, you do.

GINA: Tell me what you want to hear.

SIM: The truth!

GINA: I don't know!

SIM: Yes, you do!

GINA: *(Near tears.)* I . . . don't know, I . . . just thought it seemed like a good idea. And I guess it wasn't.

SIM: What wasn't?

GINA: I mean . . . I guess . . . everything. Troy and you and all of it. Maybe I'm too young. Maybe—

SIM: You're not! You're not. You're just not being yourself. You're sweet and honest and nice. You're not cruel and a . . . whore.

GINA: I'm not a whore!

SIM: You're acting like one!

GINA: No! I never . . . I just don't understand what you want from me. I'm sorry. I'm sorry if I made you think . . . if I made you mad and if you thought we . . . were more serious. I didn't mean to. I didn't know. I just . . . I'm sorry, Sim.

SIM: No, you're not.

GINA: Yes! You have to believe me.

SIM: I don't believe you. You never admitted—You won't say it, will you?

(GINA starts panic.)

GINA: I don't know what to say! I don't know what you want me to say!

EMILY: Sim, you're scaring her!

SIM: What do you know? Gina, I don't want to scare you. I want to understand. I want you to understand. I want you to see the truth.

EMILY: What truth?

SIM: She should be with me.

EMILY: I—I'll be your girlfriend.

JAY: Emily, shut up!

EMILY: No, I mean it, Sim. I'll be your girlfriend.

(SIM looks at EMILY.)

SIM: You just don't get it. I don't want you. I don't want anyone but Gina. I only want Gina. I loved you, Gina. And you treated me like trash.

GINA: No! I never thought that.

SIM: You did. And all I ever wanted was to be with you.

TROY: Listen, man, she's just a girl—

GINA: Thanks a lot, Troy!

TROY: I'm just saying you shouldn't get all caught up in knots—

SIM: See? He doesn't care about you. I'm the only one who cares about you.

GINA: OK.

SIM: OK, what?

GINA: I'll be your girlfriend. Again. I'll be your girlfriend again. You're right, Sim. I see that now. You're the right guy for me. I was stupid before. I don't know what I was thinking. You were good to me. I'm sorry I didn't see that. I'm sorry I wasn't good enough to you. I don't deserve you, I guess. I guess that's what I thought, that I didn't deserve you. But if you want me . . . again . . . I'll be your girlfriend. I really want to see you again, Sim. Please? Let's work this out.

SIM: You don't mean it.

GINA: I do. I swear.

SIM: No, you don't. You don't think you're not good enough for me. You think you're too good for me.

GINA: No. Not at all. I swear.

SIM: I'm sick of all of this.

(SIM takes a step back and raises his gun.)

SIM: I'm sick of all of you. I'm sick of everything.

TALK BACK!

1. Who's telling the truth about the relationship, Gina or Sim?

2. How do you think you'd react if you were pushed to the edge?

3. How do you think you'd react in a life or death situation like the one in Scene 2?

4. Have you ever felt betrayed or belittled by someone? How did you react?

5. Have you ever been stalked? What can you do to protect yourself in that situation?

6. Was Troy justified in beating up Sim if he was truly stalking Gina?

7. What is mob mentality? Do you think it exists? What do you think sparks a mob?

8. What should you do when you find yourself in a destructive, unbalanced relationship?

HOW I SEE IT

3F, 2M

WHO

FEMALES	MALES
Aimee	Del
Keysha	Marlon
Stina

WHERE Scene 1: A high school girls' bathroom; Scene 2: A high school hallway.

WHEN Present day.

When you're with your friends, pay attention to their eye contact with you. How often do they look you in the eyes? When do they look away? Does looking away indicate disinterest or something else? Bring what you learn to your performance.

Examine (through writing) a problem you either fear or are totally unfamiliar with. Here are some ideas: being sued, being responsible for an accident, winning the lottery, getting kicked out of your house.

Scene 1: Blue

STINA: What's going on in there, Aimee?

KEYSHA: What do you think's going on in there?

AIMEE: *(From offstage.)* Just a minute!

KEYSHA: Come on, Aimee, don't keep us in suspense!

AIMEE: *(From offstage.)* Hold on, hold on! I'll be there in a minute!

STINA: All you have to do is pee on it!

AIMEE: *(From offstage.)* I know! Shut up!

STINA: My mother was so mad at me when I thought I was pregnant. She yelled for, like, three days straight. Like I didn't feel bad or scared enough without her doing that. I was like, "Thanks a lot for the support, Mom, this is so helpful!" She totally didn't get it. But then I wasn't pregnant after all, so it was OK.

KEYSHA: It happens. What are you gonna do?

STINA: Well, if you ask my mom, what I'm supposed to do now is avoid boys for the entire rest of your existence and become, like, a nun. I'm supposed to change my whole life and who I am so this never happens again. God forbid she actually got me birth control or something like that. Something normal and reasonable. No. I'm not supposed to have a life. As if I could give up guys!

KEYSHA: You? No way.

STINA: I know! **I was chasing them since I was in diapers, practically. And I always catch them, too.**

KEYSHA: No one would say you aren't fast.

STINA: **Hey, shut up! I can't help it if guys like me back. Don't judge me, Keysha. I'm no slut.**

KEYSHA: I didn't say you were.

STINA: **I just happen to like guys. Who doesn't?**

KEYSHA: Lesbians.

STINA: I could never be a lesbian.

KEYSHA: You wouldn't get pregnant.

STINA: That's true. Could you kiss a girl?

KEYSHA: I don't know. Maybe. If I had a few drinks.

STINA: You'd kiss anyone after a few drinks.

KEYSHA: Don't remind me.

STINA: Hurry up, Aimee! Did you fall in or something? Class is going to start any minute.

KEYSHA: As if you'd be sorry to miss class.

(AIMEE enters.)

AIMEE: OK, OK. What does this mean? It says that I should see a blue line and it's like a blob.

STINA: What color is it?

AIMEE: Blue.

KEYSHA: Your mom is gonna kill you.

AIMEE: But it's a blob!

STINA: You could take another.

AIMEE: Another test? I don't have the money for another one.

KEYSHA: It's blue, though. Blue means it's positive.

AIMEE: But it's a *blob*, Keysha. Not a line.

KEYSHA: Does that matter, Stina? What did yours look like?

STINA: Well, mine looked pink.

AIMEE: Was it a line?

STINA: It was a blob, too.

KEYSHA: But it was pink.

STINA: Kinda magenta.

KEYSHA: But definitely not blue.

STINA: No. Not really. I mean it had some blue in it, but it wasn't blue. Plus, I got my period the next day.

AIMEE: Maybe I will, too.

KEYSHA: I hate to tell you this, sweetie, but it looks like you're pregnant.

AIMEE: Great.

STINA: What are you gonna do?

KEYSHA: You need to tell Del.

AIMEE: What does he care?

STINA: He might want to know.

KEYSHA: You want to keep it or not?

AIMEE: I don't know. I never thought this would happen.

STINA: You knew it could happen.

AIMEE: Of course I knew it *could* happen. I just didn't think it *would*. And it's not even like it was worth it. I don't even think I like Del anymore.

KEYSHA: You'd better start to like him again. He's the daddy, right?

AIMEE: Well, right.

STINA: Could it be anyone else?

AIMEE: No.

STINA: You're sure?

AIMEE: Positive. One hundred percent. It couldn't be anyone else.

KEYSHA: So, are you gonna tell him?

AIMEE: I don't know. Can't we just slow down? This isn't the kind of thing you make split decisions about.

KEYSHA: But you don't have forever either.

STINA: OK. Let's talk this through. Do you know if you want to have a baby or not? Keep in mind that if you don't, there's no changing your mind once it's done. And if you do, you either have to give it away or you have to take care of it forever.

AIMEE: I think I want to have it. I don't think I could kill it.

STINA: I could. I'd hate to have a baby.

KEYSHA: I'd have the baby. I don't know if I could give it away, though. But I don't think I could take care of it.

AIMEE: I think I could take care of it. I think I could take real good care of it.

STINA: What is your mom gonna think?

AIMEE: It's not her baby.

STINA: But you live with her. You're under her roof. I'm just telling you the stuff my mom said.

AIMEE: But I'd take care of the baby.

STINA: But who's gonna pay to feed it?

AIMEE: I could get a job.

STINA: Then you couldn't take care of it.

AIMEE: How much could a baby cost? It's so little.

KEYSHA: Diapers, food—I don't know.

STINA: Well, again, if we believe my mom, a lot.

AIMEE: I've babysat my whole life. I could take care of a baby. I think I want it.

STINA: No parties anymore. Unless your mom is way cooler than mine.

AIMEE: You know she's not.

KEYSHA: We'll miss you, Aimee!

STINA: Don't have it, Aimee.

AIMEE: We don't even know for sure I'm pregnant.

STINA: True. I think you should take another test. Or wait a little while longer and just see what happens.

KEYSHA: Should we go to class then?

AIMEE: Go get Del. I want to talk to him.

KEYSHA: Are you serious?

STINA: That's a huge mistake.

KEYSHA: But I guess he should know.

STINA: But even she doesn't know for sure.

AIMEE: Look, I just want to talk to him. I need to figure out if I want to break up with him.

KEYSHA: But what if you *are* pregnant? Don't you want to try to stay together with him?

STINA: Look, these scares go on all the time. Let's not jump to conclusions. Just look at what happened to me. Nothing! Looking back, it would have been better if I'd just kept my mouth shut instead of telling my mom.

KEYSHA: But what if you were pregnant? Wouldn't you want her to know?

AIMEE: You could have pretended to get really fat.

STINA: Actually, I did think that. I just thought I'd wear baggy clothes.

AIMEE: But you told her.

STINA: She's so nosy. She would have found out anyway, I figured.

AIMEE: Go get Del, Keysha, please? He's probably by his locker.

KEYSHA: OK.

AIMEE: But don't tell him anything, OK? I don't think I'm going to tell him anything, since we don't know for sure . . . I just want to talk to him, OK?

KEYSHA: OK.

(KEYSHA exits.)

AIMEE: Seriously, Stina, what do you think I should do?

STINA: I just know what I'd do.

AIMEE: What?

STINA: Get rid of it. Tell no one. Except you guys, of course. Just pretend like it never happened.

AIMEE: I don't know if I can. I'll think of it like a baby, I know it.

STINA: Think of it like a nose job. You're getting rid of something that makes your life difficult.

AIMEE: That's a terrible thing to say about a baby.

STINA: But it's true. I hate to say it, but my mom was right about one thing. We can't have a baby. We can't take care of it or pay for it. And I know that I, personally, wouldn't want to give up dating and parties and all that. I'm glad I wasn't pregnant.

AIMEE: But if you're so glad, how come you don't do anything different now?

STINA: Like give up guys? That's unrealistic. I'm just more careful now.

AIMEE: I don't know. This has turned me off guys completely.

STINA: I doubt that.

(KEYSHA enters.)

KEYSHA: Del is outside. He was real suspicious.

AIMEE: Tell him to come in.

KEYSHA: It's the girl's room, Aimee.

STINA: So what?

KEYSHA: So . . . Fine. I'll bring him in. Just don't be surprised if it gets around that he was in here with you.

AIMEE: Like that's my biggest problem.

KEYSHA: True. Listen, Aimee, sweetie, we're here for you, OK?

AIMEE: OK.

STINA: Come on, Keysha, let's go.

KEYSHA: If you need us, we'll be outside.

STINA: Unless someone comes along. Then we'll be hiding in the stairwell.

AIMEE: 'K.

(KEYSHA and STINA exit; DEL enters.)

DEL: What's this about? I'm supposed to be in class.

AIMEE: I think we just need to talk.

DEL: Now?

AIMEE: Yeah.

DEL: So talk, I guess.

AIMEE: Do you like me?

DEL: Well, yeah.

AIMEE: Do you want to see other girls?

DEL: I like you.

AIMEE: What . . . what do you . . . Do you think we have a good time?

DEL: Yeah. Pretty good.

AIMEE: Do you . . . I mean, what would you do if . . . do you see us being together for a long time?

DEL: Dunno.

AIMEE: Would you help me if I were in trouble?

DEL: Like what? You're acting crazy. I gotta go to class.

(DEL starts to leave.)

AIMEE: What if I was pregnant?

DEL: What? Are you pregnant?

AIMEE: I don't know.

DEL: This is crazy. I don't want to talk to you.

AIMEE: Answer the question.

DEL: If you're pregnant, it's not by me. It must be some other guy. You must be seeing some other guy.

AIMEE: No. I'm not seeing anyone but you.

DEL: I didn't make you pregnant. We . . . I barely . . . Why are you talking about this? I'm not going to marry you if that's what you think. I'm a kid. So you can just forget it. I don't want to have any babies. Not for a long, long time, if ever. So, I don't know what this is about, but I did not make you pregnant and I don't . . . I don't like you that much. So whatever you're thinking, you can just forget it.

AIMEE: I'm not thinking anything.

DEL: You must be thinking something, or you wouldn't bring it up. Otherwise, that's just sick. This whole thing is a sick conversation and I'm done

with it. You do whatever. But I don't want anything . . . There's just no way—

AIMEE: No way you could make me pregnant?

DEL: No way I could be a father.

AIMEE: Why not?

DEL: Because I just couldn't. No way.

AIMEE: It's possible.

DEL: It's not. I'm outta here.

    (DEL leaves.)

Scene 2: Happy

MARLON: *(To KEYSHA.)* So, do you want to go out tomorrow?

(AIMEE enters. She is now definitely, visibly pregnant.)

AIMEE: Keysha, are we still on for tomorrow? I'm getting popcorn and ice cream and the works. I rented a bunch of movies—you like comedies, right?

KEYSHA: Well, about that, Aimee, I was thinking about going out with Marlon.

AIMEE: Oh. But I thought we were all set. We planned this last week.

KEYSHA: I just thought that since we were just going to your house . . .

MARLON: It's OK. I'll just catch you later then.

KEYSHA: No, don't go, Marlon. I mean, just hold on a second.

AIMEE: You know what? Never mind.

KEYSHA: You mean it? I mean, I love you, Aimee, and I wouldn't mind watching movies at your house . . .

AIMEE: No. Never mind. It's doesn't matter. Another time.

KEYSHA: You're sure?

AIMEE: Yeah.

KEYSHA: Thanks, Aimee!

(KEYSHA and MARLON exit. DEL enters.)

DEL: Hi.

AIMEE: You don't have to talk to me.

DEL: I know. I don't want to talk to you. But my dad and mom say I have to since your mom told them I was the father of your baby.

AIMEE: I didn't tell her to do that.

DEL: Well, she did.

AIMEE: I don't need a father for this baby. I can do this myself.

DEL: Well, tell your mother that.

AIMEE: I did.

DEL: Now my parents are making me get a job so I can give you money.

AIMEE: Well, it is your baby, too, I guess.

DEL: It's your fault you got pregnant. I don't want a job.

AIMEE: Tell your parents that.

DEL: I did.

(Beat.)

DEL: Why don't you just get rid of it?

AIMEE: Because I want this baby. It's not an "it." Plus, it's too late.

DEL: Why did you have to do this? Why did you have to ruin my life?

AIMEE: I'm the one having it.

DEL: Well your choice is ruining my life. That isn't right.

AIMEE: I guess that's too bad. Because I'm going to love this baby even if you don't.

DEL: You are so stupid. You just don't get it. Kids aren't supposed to have kids. I don't want a kid. I don't want anything to do with you or this baby. I'm still not convinced it's mine. How am I supposed to know?

AIMEE: Because I'm telling you it's yours. I don't know why you can't believe this is your baby. You know what you did, what we did. Unless you are really ignorant, you know that it's possible that I can be pregnant. So stop trying to pretend it's not or pretend that I'm some kind of slut. I made a mistake. *We* made a mistake. And now we have to deal with it. I'm going to have a baby. That's just a fact. Deal with it. Or don't! I don't care. I'm going to do this with or without you. I'm the mother. Of course, if you want to help, that's great! And it shows how decent your parents are since they want to help.

DEL: I just can't believe you want this thing.

AIMEE: This *baby*. And I do want it.

DEL: Why?

AIMEE: I want this baby because I can love it. Because he or she can love me. Because I know now that I'll never be alone. That's why I don't need you. That's why I don't need anyone anymore except my baby. And my mom, I guess. So you can come or you can go. Just leave me and my baby be. Because we are going to be happy.

DEL: Whatever. Just tell your mother not to call my house anymore. I don't want any part of it. I don't believe you anyway. I hate you. I just can't believe you'd do something this stupid to me.

AIMEE: I didn't do anything to you.

DEL: Yes, you did. I wish I could just get rid of it, get rid of you.

AIMEE: Are you threatening me?

DEL: No. Just . . . leave me alone.

(*DEL exits. STINA enters.*)

STINA: Are you OK?

AIMEE: Yeah.

STINA: We saw him talking to you. What was he saying?

AIMEE: Nothing, really.

STINA: He's mad.

AIMEE: I know. I'm not too bothered by him.

STINA: Do you mean that?

AIMEE: What do you mean?

STINA: I mean, I wonder if you're not more upset than you show.

AIMEE: Why is it so hard to believe that I could be happy?

STINA: Because you're pregnant and in high school.

AIMEE: So what?

STINA: So to most people, that would *not* be good.

AIMEE: I guess I'm not most people.

STINA: What do you like so much about it?

AIMEE: I just keep thinking that I'm bringing new life into the world. And that I have a purpose. All this time, I was wondering what my purpose was. Why I was living. Now I know why. I was supposed to get pregnant. I'm supposed to have this baby. I'm supposed to be a mother. I can show someone love and give the love I have to give. Does that make any sense to you?

STINA: I guess it does. I do kinda understand, I just think for myself that's what I might want to do when I'm, like, twenty-five or thirty. Not now.

AIMEE: Well, that's how I see it. I see it happening now. And I think I'm lucky that everything's coming to me so soon.

STINA: Doesn't it bother you that there's no dad?

AIMEE: I'd rather Del wasn't around. He's more trouble than help. He doesn't get it.

STINA: But if it was a good father, the right father, wouldn't that be better than having to raise the baby yourself?

AIMEE: My mother raised me herself. It's almost like a tradition now. She's a strong woman and she raised me herself. Now it's my turn to do the same thing.

STINA: I hope you still feel this way when the baby comes and it's crying all the time.

AIMEE: I probably won't always be totally happy, but it won't mean that I regret my decision.

STINA: **You know . . . it's going to be hard to be your friend a little.**

AIMEE: I know.

STINA: I just want to say that now. Because I don't want you to be upset later that I never see you.

AIMEE: I know.

STINA: It's just that I don't want to have a baby, you know? So I just don't think I'll want to be around your baby all the time. I'd rather just be a kid still. That's why I don't even babysit. I don't like responsibility. I don't want to be an adult. Actually, I want to thank you, Aimee.

AIMEE: Why?

STINA: I kind of get it now. I really see, firsthand, the mistakes I have to watch out for. No offense. I don't mean to make it sound like—

AIMEE: I know I made a mistake. I just think it will turn out for the best in the end.

STINA: Well, for me it would be a big mistake. So now I see that I have to be a lot more careful. I have to think about things more. Because I know I definitely don't want . . . I couldn't handle it, myself. I can't feed or dress or take care of myself all that too well; I'd be a wreck trying to do it for someone else. I'm just not cut out for motherhood and I don't think I will be for a *very* long time. If ever. So I'd better make sure it won't happen. Like you said way back in the beginning, you just never think it will happen to you. Now I know it can! I guess you're a role model already.

AIMEE: Excellent.

STINA: I just wanted to apologize in advance and let you know it's not you.

AIMEE: I'll miss you.

STINA: I'll miss you, too. So . . . you're going to name the baby after me, right?

AIMEE: Not a chance.

STINA: You won't name it after Del, will you?

AIMEE: No way!

STINA: What then?

AIMEE: I'll just see what name seems right. I guess I'll play it by ear.

TALK BACK!

1. If you found yourself in Aimee or Del's situation, would you want to be a parent? What option would you choose: keep the baby, put the baby up for adoption, or abort the fetus? Would this be a hard or easy decision for you?

2. Where do your parents stand on the issue of teen sex? Do you think they are right? Realistic? Too strict or too lenient? Why?

3. If you were Aimee's friend, do you think your relationship would change after she became pregnant? If so, how?

4. What do you think about Del? Can you understand his position? Do you think he's justified or a jerk?

5. Do you think you could be a single parent? What makes it difficult to be a single parent?

6. What would be the ideal set up for a family? For example, how old would the parent(s) be when the kids were born? How many kids would there be? How much money would they have?

7. What are the most important traits of a good parent and why?

WHY I DID IT

3F, 5M

WHO

FEMALES
- Holly
- Janet
- Nova

MALES
- Enrico
- Fritz
- Tyriq
- Ford
- Jacob

WHERE Scene 1: A memorial site; Scene 2: An officelike room.

WHEN The near future.

🎭 Scene 1: Everything should seem normal and relaxed until Ford's appearance, so what comes afterward has a greater impact. Scene 2: Everyone who speaks to Jacob should be very clear about their objective (what they want from him).

✎ I read in the newspaper about a writer researching why kids around the world join terrorist organizations. It got me thinking about it. That's where this play came from. Try exploring the personal background of a person who does something seemingly unthinkable. Here are some examples: murder, prostitution, kidnapping, torture. Whether it's right or wrong, there's a reason behind everything.

Scene 1: Terrorism

HOLLY: This project is boring.

ENRICO: I know. Once you see the memorial, what more is there to do?

JACOB: I guess we can stare at it some more.

(Beat.)

ENRICO: What are we supposed to be getting out of this? It's a bunch of names.

HOLLY: Well, I guess it's sad that all these people died.

ENRICO: Of course that's sad.

JACOB: Maybe if we try to think of all these names as people.

HOLLY: There are a lot of them.

ENRICO: It's weird to think about. It's hard to imagine.

JACOB: It's depressing.

HOLLY: It's too sad. I don't want to think about it. Let's talk about something else. Tell me something I don't know about you, Enrico.

ENRICO: When I was, like, eleven my sister closed the car door on my leg. Really slammed it hard. I re-member it so well. I think she did it on purpose. My sister hates me. I think she finds it fun to torture me. She gets this crazy look in her eye, like she's about to laugh, but she's also mad at me. She's a wacko. So that day we're coming home from seeing my grand-parents, and she gets out of the car first. Normally, I'd get out of the other side of the car, but there's this huge puddle next to my door, so I slide over in the seat. She opens the door and looks at me, I swear, she looks at me with that laughing, angry look and slams the door shut with all her might. There was this moment where I knew exactly what was happen-ing, but I couldn't do anything. And I was sure my leg would break in half.

JACOB: So? Did it?

ENRICO: It didn't. I just had a huge bruise, and it swelled up and hurt really bad. She swore to my par-ents it was an accident. But I knew. I saw that look. She did it on purpose.

HOLLY: That's terrible!

ENRICO: That's my sister.

HOLLY: Now it's your turn, Jacob.

JACOB: I've got nothing to tell. My life is boring.

HOLLY: That's not true.

JACOB: Sure it is!

ENRICO: (Kidding.) He really is boring.

JACOB: Shut up, Enrico.

ENRICO: You said it first!

JACOB: No, I didn't!

ENRICO: Yes, you did.

HOLLY: Yeah, you did.

JACOB: Well, I guess it is. I'm an ordinary guy.

HOLLY: I don't believe you have nothing at all to say. Tell me one thing you think.

JACOB: I think?

HOLLY: Like an opinion about something.

JACOB: OK. Well, I saw this story the other day about a guy who was attacked by a chimpanzee or something. Like, really horribly attacked. And I just have to think, why would someone ever have a wild animal around him on purpose? Like I also saw a story about a guy having a tiger and an alligator in his apartment. What was he thinking? It seems to me that these animals are wild because they're supposed to be *in* the wild. You know? They're not supposed to be in your house. And you probably shouldn't be surprised if they bite your arm off or anything. Like even snakes. Lots of people have snakes. Get a clue, people! Snakes bite you. They're not cuddly or sweet or gentle. So leave them alone! Honestly, you almost deserve what you get when you do something like that. That's just crazy. If I ever get that crazy, like adopting a grizzly bear, will you stop me? You gotta wonder what drives people to that. How desperate must you be?

HOLLY: OK, not exactly a happier story.

ENRICO: Evil animals instead of evil sisters.

JACOB: But that's just it. The animals are just being themselves, right?

HOLLY: But I can see why you could think an animal was gentle and sweet, then one day they go nuts and you're totally surprised.

JACOB: That's my point! They're *wild animals*. We should just leave them alone.

ENRICO: How did we even get on this topic?

JACOB: Holly asked me to talk about something.

ENRICO: And that's the something you picked?

JACOB: That's the first thing that came to mind.

ENRICO: That's the first thing that came to mind? That's weird, man. Seriously.

(Beat.)

HOLLY: It's so quiet here.

JACOB: I'm surprised no one else is here.

ENRICO: I saw some kids on the way here.

HOLLY: Maybe they have a school project, too.

JACOB: Well, why aren't they here then?

HOLLY: How should I know? What am I, psychic?

ENRICO: Doesn't seem like it.

HOLLY: I knew you were going to say that.

ENRICO: Ha, ha.

(FORD enters suddenly.)

FORD: What are you doing here?

JACOB: What do you mean?

FORD: I mean, what are you doing here?

HOLLY: We're doing a school project.

FORD: You shouldn't be here.

ENRICO: Why?

FORD: This isn't where you should be.

JACOB: Says who?

FORD: Says us. This is our area. We own this place.

ENRICO: You don't own it. It doesn't have your name on it.

FORD: Sure it does.

ENRICO: Where?

FORD: We don't need to write it down.

HOLLY: We're just doing a project.

JACOB: If it makes you feel any better, we're not enjoying it.

FORD: I'm not being funny.

ENRICO: Take it easy.

FORD: You don't tell me what to do.

HOLLY: Can we all just calm down? We're just doing a project. We're not hurting anyone. And we're done now.

(FORD leaves.)

ENRICO: **I don't want to leave just because he said to leave.**

JACOB: Who is he to tell us what to do?

HOLLY: Well, we are in occupied territory.

JACOB: But we're not doing anything and it's before curfew.

ENRICO: I don't know why we're supposed to be researching and trying to understand these people. That kid was just a bully.

HOLLY: It doesn't mean they all are.

JACOB: Who cares? Let's get out of here.

ENRICO: I don't want that kid to think he scared us off.

HOLLY: But we're done anyway.

JACOB: Yeah. It's just boring.

ENRICO: But it's the principle. I don't want anyone to think he can push me around. I don't get it. This is a place. A piece of land. How can anyone own it? I don't even get countries. It's all just blobs of land. How come people get so patriotic? It's not like we choose where we come from. We were just born into it. Why should anyone be proud or ashamed of where they were born? You have no control over it. It all just seems weird to me. I don't see why people get so worked up. We're all just people, right? Whatever color, whatever blob of land we were born on, whatever language we speak, it's all the same.

JACOB: Thanks for the inspirational message.

ENRICO: I mean it. I know it's clichéd, but it's true, right? In the end we're the same. And I can see how someone could get upset if I was robbing him or something, but I'm just standing here. Doing nothing. How can that be wrong?

HOLLY: But that's just it. It's the robbing thing. People are fighting over who owns the land.

ENRICO: But unless your house is on it, who cares who owns every little piece of earth?

HOLLY: I guess they do.

JACOB: Who are "they"?

HOLLY: Most people.

ENRICO: I don't get it.

   (Beat.)

JACOB: What's that?

HOLLY: What's what?

JACOB: That noise.

ENRICO: I don't hear anything.

JACOB: I hear something. It's quiet, but it sounds like it's coming closer.

Scene 2: Terrorist

TYRIQ: They killed your friends Holly and Enrico, didn't they?

JACOB: Yeah. They got blown up.

TYRIQ: You see? They want to kill us. All of us. We have to protect ourselves. Do you want that to happen again? To your mother? Your sister?

JACOB: No.

TYRIQ: How did you feel when you watched your friends die?

JACOB: Confused.

TYRIQ: Why?

JACOB: I didn't understand . . . I didn't know what was happening or why anyone would do that. I just don't know why anyone would do that. It was horrible. Horrible.

TYRIQ: You watched them suffer.

JACOB: I couldn't . . . I didn't know what to do. But I couldn't help them. And there was no one around. Except . . . there wasn't anyone around who would help. And it was too late. I couldn't do anything for Enrico. He was dead right away. Holly . . . Holly cried. And she screamed in a way that I've never heard before. But I couldn't do anything. I just didn't know what to do. It was just so horrible. I don't understand . . . Holly and

Enrico were my friends. They were nice, good people. They shouldn't have died. It wasn't fair. They didn't do anything to anyone. I don't know why anyone would want to kill a bunch of kids.

TYRIQ: Don't you see? They don't care. They don't care about people. You were in their way. So they removed you.

JACOB: I knew . . . They told us to go, but we didn't listen. I didn't listen. We didn't think . . . We should've left. I wish we'd left. I don't understand any of this.

TYRIQ: Because it's wrong, Jacob. What they did is wrong. You should be allowed to go anywhere you want. We're about freedom, Jacob. No one should be killed because they were in the wrong place. It wasn't your fault.

JACOB: It was. I should have gotten them to leave. And I heard the rocket before it came. I didn't know what it was, but I heard something. I could have done something.

TYRIQ: You can't know what's in these monsters' minds, Jacob. Bottom line is, what they did was wrong.

JACOB: I know. I know. But then . . . why . . . How is what you do any different, Tyriq?

TYRIQ: Because we're about justice. We're about freedom. We're about stopping violence.

JACOB: I don't know. I just want to . . . I just want to go home.

(NOVA and JANET enter.)

NOVA: Tyriq? They need you next door.

TYRIQ: Of course. We'll talk more later, Jacob, OK?

JACOB: I guess.

(TYRIQ exits.)

NOVA: Hi, Jacob. We've heard a lot about you.

JACOB: Hi.

NOVA: I'm Nova and this is Janet.

JACOB: Hi.

JANET: Can we get you anything?

JACOB: No.

NOVA: We want you to feel comfortable.

JACOB: I—don't care. I don't care about any of this. I just want to go home and sleep.

JANET: And then what, Jacob?

JACOB: What do you mean? I don't know.

JANET: After you wake up, everything will be the same.

JACOB: I know that.

NOVA: We don't want to make you feel bad. Exactly the opposite. We want to help you. We want to help you make things right.

JACOB: How can anything be right? My friends are dead.

JANET: And no one can change that.

JACOB: I know!

JANET: But you can make sure it doesn't happen again. To any of your friends. To your family. To anyone else's friends.

JACOB: I don't want to talk to you. Leave me alone. I just want to be alone.

NOVA: You're angry, Jacob.

JACOB: Of course I'm angry!

NOVA: So do something, Jacob!

JACOB: Like what?

JANET: We know your pain. We feel your pain.

JACOB: No, you don't.

JANET: We do! Why do you think we're here? My mother was beaten severely. Her brother was shot. Tyriq lost his whole family. We know what you're going through. We can help you.

NOVA: We can show you how to take it back. Take back your power. Fight back! You can't just sit back anymore, Jacob. You're part of this fight. These people need to be stopped.

JACOB: What am I supposed to do? I'm just one person! I'm just a kid.

JANET: You need to fight back.

NOVA: We know it doesn't always seem to make sense. But we live in a crazy world. We live in a world where violence is forced on us.

JANET: We need to fight back. It's the only way. Do you see that?

JACOB: I don't know. Yes. I guess so. I don't know what to think. I just want all of this not to be true.

JANET: But it is true.

JACOB: I know that!

(FRITZ enters.)

FRITZ: Can I talk to Jacob for a minute?

NOVA: Of course.

JANET: Jacob, if you need to talk, just ask for us, Janet and Nova.

NOVA: We're here for you. We understand. We do.

(JANET and NOVA exit.)

FRITZ: You're got a lot of people telling you a lot of things.

(Beat.)

FRITZ: It must be overwhelming.

JACOB: My friends just died. They were killed. They were blown to pieces.

FRITZ: What Janet and Nova said is true. We, every one of us, have gone through just what you're going through. Terrible things. Unbelievable things.

JACOB: How do you know what they said to me?

FRITZ: I know Nova and Janet. They're great people. You'll like them. We thought maybe you might want to talk to them. They're easy to talk to and really nice. (Beat.) **This is a real moment for you, Jacob. I don't know if you know it. This is an event. This is a time when you are going to make a huge decision about your life, whether you want to sit back and let life happen to you or if you want to do something, make an impact.**

JACOB: I just want to go to sleep.

FRITZ: **Don't you see? You can't sleep anymore. You can't close your eyes. You're no longer innocent. Do you know what you'll see in your sleep? Enrico and Holly being killed. There won't be any rest, Jacob. You can't escape what happened. You can't turn away from it. There will be no rest. And what good would that do your friends? How will their deaths have meaning if you just look away,** close your eyes? You can't let them die for nothing. And you can't let those people win. Do you see that?

JACOB: I don't know. I don't know what—I don't want to see anything.

FRITZ: You have no choice.

JACOB: I know.

FRITZ: You have to fight. We have to stop them. We can't let them take over. We can't let them destroy our family and our friends.

JACOB: But I don't want to kill anyone. And I don't want to die, too.

FRITZ: It's possible that people will be sacrificed. But those people die with honor. Because they fight for what's right.

JACOB: Are you saying I'm going to die?

FRITZ: I don't know what's going to happen to anyone. You might die. We all die sometime. I'm just saying that for me, I would rather die fighting for what's right rather than accepting a wrong. I cannot stand to watch another innocent person die. And if that means I have to sacrifice, if that means I have to sometimes be brutal in my methods to stop this insanity, then that's what I will do. I don't know about you, Jacob, but I can't stand by and watch people like your friends die any more. I want to take action.

(Beat.)

FRITZ: Join us, Jacob. We know what you're going through. We understand you. And we're here to see that none of this ever happens again. Join us.

(Beat.)

JACOB: OK. I will.

FRITZ: Good. I can see that you care about your friends and your family.

JACOB: I don't want to see anybody else die.

FRITZ: Then there's something we need you to do, Jacob.

JACOB: What?

FRITZ: An assignment. Are you ready for it?

JACOB: Yes.

TALK BACK!

1. Do you agree or disagree with Enrico's political beliefs?

2. When you are threatened or forbidden to do something, are you likely to obey or rebel?

3. Did you make any judgments about which side was right and which side was wrong? Do you have enough information to make an assessment? If not, what else would you want to know?

4. What do you think of Tyriq, Janet, Nova, and Fritz? Are they good or bad people?

5. What do you think your instinct would be if you were Jacob? What would you want to do at the beginning of Scene 2 and why?

6. Fight fire with fire. What do you think of this statement? Is it true or false? Are there other options? Why or why not?

7. Is there any cause that you think you might sacrifice your life for? Is anything worth dying for?

THE OTHER ONE

5F, 4M

WHO

FEMALES	MALES
Joan	Dom
Nicki	Howie
Pop	Mac
Sabrina	Willis
Zinnie	

WHERE Anywhere.

WHEN Present day.

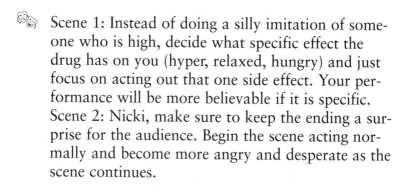 Scene 1: Instead of doing a silly imitation of someone who is high, decide what specific effect the drug has on you (hyper, relaxed, hungry) and just focus on acting out that one side effect. Your performance will be more believable if it is specific. Scene 2: Nicki, make sure to keep the ending a surprise for the audience. Begin the scene acting normally and become more angry and desperate as the scene continues.

Addiction is an issue faced by many people. Choose an addiction and write about it. See if you can make the audience understand the motivation behind it. For example, I think there is a sense of family and community among Dom's friends when they get high.

Scene 1: Trouble

WILLIS: I feel so much better.

MAC: There's nothing I hate more than not knowing where you're going to get the next hit from.

HOWIE: Dom, you're a genius. Where did the money come from, anyhow?

DOM: Do you care?

HOWIE: No.

WILLIS: I don't care about anything.

MAC: It's great.

HOWIE: It is so cool to hang out with a bunch of guys who understand, you know . . . have the same interests.

DOM: Don't get all mushy on us, Howie.

HOWIE: I'm just saying . . .

(NICKI *knocks on the door.*)

WILLIS: *(Quietly.)* Oh my God! Someone's knocking on the door!

MAC: We can all hear.

WILLIS: *(Quietly.)* Are we going to . . . should we do something?

MAC: Don't get paranoid, Willis.

DOM: Who is it?

NICKI: *(Offstage.)* It's me, stupid.

DOM: What do you want?

NICKI: *(Offstage.)* Open the door.

DOM: What do you want, midget?

HOWIE: She's a midget because she's short.

MAC: You're a genius, Howie.

NICKI: *(Offstage.)* Open the door! I want to tell you something.

DOM: No. Go away. Come back later. No, just go away.

NICKI: *(Offstage.)* Fine! I was trying to be nice, but never mind.

WILLIS: When are your parents coming home?

DOM: Not for ages.

MAC: You're sure?

DOM: Yeah.

HOWIE: So what's she want to talk to you about?

DOM: How should I know?

WILLIS: Don't you want to know? Maybe it's important.

DOM: No way. I want to relax.

MAC: So . . . I think I've got a woman.

DOM: A woman? I doubt that. I doubt you've even got a goldfish.

MAC: Come on, I'm being serious. I think she likes me.

HOWIE: No one's ever liked you.

MAC: No one's ever liked *you*.

WILLIS: Let's face it. There are not enough stoner chicks in the world. And those chicks like the jocks, anyway, like all other chicks.

DOM: Stoner chicks are not my type. They never wash their hair.

HOWIE: We don't wash our hair.

DOM: But we're *guys*. So it's OK. It's not OK for a chick to be unhygienic. Girls are supposed to paint their toenails and wash their hair. I'm not saying it's fair, I'm just saying it's true. Actually, it is fair. We're taller than girls, right? For the most part? So we have to look at the tops of their heads a lot more than they do with us. Did that make sense?

MAC: No.

DOM: I don't care. I'm just saying, we're more likely to smell their hair than they are to smell ours. And we're more likely to get a face full of greasy hair than they are. I mean, if we're kissing one of them or something. *(Beat.)* Maybe we should start a band. We don't have to actually play anything because that's why they have recording engineers. So we should do that. I think . . . I think our look fits the rock star image, right? We'd get a lot of action that way. Am I making sense?

MAC: No.

HOWIE: I'm hungry. Really hungry. Do you have anything to eat?

DOM: Nothing good.

HOWIE: We should get something.

WILLIS: We can't leave. Someone might see us.

HOWIE: So what?

MAC: So anyway, about my woman. She's hot. She likes me, for real.

DOM: Why would she like you?

MAC: I had my camera with me. She was interested. I told her I wanted to be a war photographer.

HOWIE: Do you want to be a war photographer?

MAC: I might want to be a war photographer. It

sounds cool, doesn't it? You get to go to dangerous places, but you're not actually in the army or
anything. You don't have to do anything except
take a bunch of pictures.

WILLIS: You're supposed to take pictures of horrific
things.

MAC: I could take pictures of violent stuff. It
wouldn't bother me. I've seen every movie ever
made where people say, "This movie was nasty
and disturbing! Don't ever see it. You won't be
able to handle it." I can handle anything. The
grosser the better. It doesn't bother me.

WILLIS: So if you see, like, a kid being tortured, you'd
just take pictures and be OK with it.

MAC: It does seem a little weird to think about it—
just watching things happen and not actually
doing anything to stop it. Especially if it's something really bad. That is blowing my mind. That is
so weird. I never thought about it. A war photographer just has to watch people committing
atrocities and do nothing. That is completely
weird. I never thought about it like that.

WILLIS: Told you.

DOM: You're depressing me. I need something else.

HOWIE: I'm hungry.

DOM: I'm going to check my parents' medicine cabinet.

WILLIS: You can't leave.

DOM: I can.

MAC: What's wrong with you?

WILLIS: What if your sister sees you?

DOM: Who cares?

HOWIE: You should get something to eat, too. What do you have to eat?

DOM: I told you—nothing good. My mom's on some stupid kick to keep us healthy.

MAC: That's funny.

WILLIS: Why?

MAC: 'Cause Dom is, like, the least healthy person on earth.

DOM: Why do you say that?

MAC: Are you serious? Let's see . . . you eat crap, you take drugs—

DOM: OK. But I'm not the *least* healthy person on earth, I bet. I mean, people are starving, you idiot.

MAC: Take it easy.

HOWIE: If I don't get something to eat, I'm going to die.

WILLIS: You're not going to die.

HOWIE: How do you know?

WILLIS: I know. Everyone knows. It's common sense.

HOWIE: What is?

WILLIS: That you're not going to die.

HOWIE: I'm not?

DOM: You're wasted.

HOWIE: Hey, how about we go get some chili fries?

DOM: That's fine with me as long as I get to drive.

WILLIS: You can't drive.

DOM: I can do whatever I want.

WILLIS: But you shouldn't drive.

DOM: And you should?

WILLIS: I didn't say that.

MAC: Let's just go if we're gonna go.

DOM: I don't feel any different. Let's stop off and get something else. That last stuff wasn't very good. I'm good to drive. I feel fine. I don't feel any different.

MAC: Let's go if we're gonna go.

WILLIS: How are we going to get out?

DOM: We'll walk out the door.

HOWIE: If I don't get chips, I'm going to die.

MAC: Let's go.

Scene 2: Troubled

(NICKI *walks into the room and slams the door.*)

NICKI: Why is everything so hard?

SABRINA: What are you talking about, Nicki?

NICKI: All I want is to be treated decently. And all I get is . . . they just yell at me all the time. Like everything's my fault. My brother can ruin his whole life and that's fine, but I'm not allowed to have even normal, decent—I'm just treated like I'm nothing! Did you ever just hate your parents? Just totally? Totally, totally, totally, totally? Well, I do. Just now. I hate them. Totally, totally, totally! You just cannot talk to people like that. They are so unreasonable. I—I am so mad! I just go in the kitchen and my brother, the loser, is in there blocking the refrigerator. So I ask him to move and he doesn't, he's being a total pain about it, and so I call him a loser because that's what he is. And *I* get yelled at. It's like since Dom got into trouble he's some kind of delicate flower and I have to be careful not to hurt his feelings. What crap! Ever since he got home from rehab, my life sucks!

JOAN: Can I ask you a question? And if you don't want to answer, don't. I totally understand.

NICKI: Whatever.

JOAN: What exactly happened with your brother? You've never said.

NICKI: Well, my brother is a loser. He stole money from my mom to buy drugs. And he took prescription drugs from my parents' medicine cabinet. He was addicted to a whole bunch of stuff. He'll take anything. He and his friends are complete losers. So then, like an idiot, he drove his car—that my parents *gave* to him, by the way—into a tree. Well done, idiot. And do I get a car? No. So now he's back from rehab, and we all have to tiptoe around him because we're not supposed to set him off. Like if we ever say anything less than totally positive to him, he'll become a drug addict again. Well, first of all, he's a pig! How am I supposed to be nice to him? And why? And since he knows that we're all supposed to be nice to him, he totally takes advantage of it! Plus, hello? There's a real world out there. Let's face reality. The whole world isn't going to be nice to him for being a burnt-out failure. Why should we? He should learn to face reality sometime. I just don't get why I get ignored and treated badly because my brother messed up. I'm always good. It doesn't make any sense.

POP: That majorly sucks.

NICKI: I know! Do you know that the day of the accident I actually was going to tell him that our mom was coming home early? Because I knew that he and his friends were all drugged out and I was trying to help him cover his butt? And this is the thanks I get.

ZINNIE: It's unfair. Parents can be so clueless.

NICKI: They totally don't see what this is doing to me. They don't even care. It's like I'm invisible.

POP: Well, you're not invisible since they're yelling at you.

NICKI: Right. I don't know which is worse.

JOAN: It's worse to be invisible.

SABRINA: No way! I'd love to be invisible to my parents.

JOAN: Well, I am, and it's no party. It makes you want to scream. You just want to be like, "Can you just be parents for five minutes? Could you help me with anything in my whole life?" It gets really boring having to figure everything out for yourself. If I didn't have friends, I swear I'd think that babies were dropped down on your front porch by storks. Honestly, my parents are so unhelpful.

NICKI: It just sucks having this brother who's like a special case. The whole world revolves around him. And he can mess up all he wants and it only seems to help him. He only gets more attention and more concern.

POP: I know what that's like, only different. My sister is perfect. She can do no wrong. She's popular and pretty and smart—gag. Completely revolting. She's, like, a cheerleader and a beauty queen. You've seen those pictures at my house. And the thing is, my parent's think she's great. And I get, "Why can't you be more like Lori?" It's like a broken record. They should make a recording of it for when I go to college so I won't miss them too much. The irony is, the last thing I'd want in the entire world is to be a cheerleading beauty queen. It's vile.

SABRINA: Is that ironic?

POP: I think so. Who knows? I'm the dumb kid. Ask my sister.

ZINNIE: So our lives suck. What now?

NICKI: I bet if I took drugs my parents would disown me.

JOAN: Have any of you ever taken any drugs?

POP: Well, weed.

SABRINA: Yeah, me too.

JOAN: You, too? I can't see that at all.

SABRINA: Why not? I'm not a total dweeb.

POP: Sure you are!

SABRINA: Ha, ha, ha.

NICKI: One time I ate all the Flintstones vitamins. Didn't do anything, though.

POP: What did you do that for?

NICKI: They tasted good, and I was mad that I was only allowed to eat one.

JOAN: One time when I was little, my mom had these laxatives that looked like chocolates in a drawer and I ate all of them!

ZINNIE: Oh no you didn't!

JOAN: I did! It was horrible! It was, like, everywhere! I was so sick!

POP: Man, that is so disgusting!

JOAN: I know! I remember I was really little and I was so scared I was dying. And there was this mess and I didn't know which was worse: dying or not cleaning up after myself! I couldn't decide whether I wanted to lie down and croak or clean up before my mom found out!

ZINNIE: That is the worst story I ever heard!

JOAN: Isn't it? It's funny now, but then . . .

SABRINA: Maybe you'll laugh at your story sometime, too, Nicki.

NICKI: Not likely. I just feel like I have to do something to make my parents understand how stupid they are. How stupid my brother is!

POP: Like what?

NICKI: Maybe I should look around my brother's room. He says he's clean, but I bet he's not. I wouldn't put it past him.

POP: You would hate it if he snuck into your stuff.

NICKI: But I'm not a drug addict.

SABRINA: Still . . .

NICKI: Well, then, maybe I'll just kill him. Then I'd get some attention and get rid of him at the same time.

JOAN: You're kidding, right?

NICKI: Of course I am. But it seriously makes you think about taking drugs when you see what great treatment you get from doing it. My brother gets the red carpet rolled out for him. As long as you're a total loser, your parents will do everything for you. Nice lesson.

ZINNIE: You're really angry.

NICKI: You're saying that like I'm being unreasonable. I have every reason to be angry.

ZINNIE: Yeah, but you're *really* angry.

NICKI: So?

SABRINA: What's that on your arm, Nicki?

NICKI: What? Oh, nothing.

POP: Nicki, are you doing heroin or something?

NICKI: Don't be stupid. I told you, I'm still the good kid trying to do everything right. Who knows why. I'm such an idiot.

SABRINA: Seriously, Nicki. What's going on with you? Zinnie's right, you're acting a little weird.

NICKI: How am I acting weird? I'm mad at my parents,

just like the rest of you. How am I any weirder than the rest of you weirdos?

ZINNIE: You're cutting yourself.

SABRINA: Is that what that is?

ZINNIE: Yeah.

NICKI: How do you know?

ZINNIE: I've seen it.

NICKI: Where?

ZINNIE: On TV.

NICKI: So that makes you an expert?

ZINNIE: No. But what else could it be?

NICKI: It could be nothing, like I said.

POP: Nick, come on. You can tell us.

NICKI: There's nothing to tell.

SABRINA: There are other ways to get attention, you know.

NICKI: Thanks, doc. It's great to know I have friends who know everything. Congratulations.

ZINNIE: Don't be like this.

NICKI: Like what?

SABRINA: Like crazy. Like mad.

NICKI: You guys are just like my parents. Why don't you just get lost?

POP: Calm down.

NICKI: Calm down? You make accusations and call me crazy—

SABRINA: I didn't mean it like that. I just meant out of proportion.

NICKI: Oh, yeah. That's better. Look, you don't know about proportion. You don't know me, and you don't understand me, obviously. So why don't you shut up and get out.

POP: Nicki—

NICKI: Get out now.

ZINNIE: We're not—

NICKI: Get out!

SABRINA: Nicki, we're only trying to—

NICKI: Don't even say "help." Because that's a huge lie. Just get out of here and get out of my life. Please. I think *you* guys are crazy. Go screw yourselves.

POP: Fine.

(POP exits, followed reluctantly by SABRINA and ZINNIE.)

JOAN: Nicki . . .

NICKI: What?

JOAN: I don't know. Just remember that . . . well, don't
be embarrassed. I took all of my mom's laxatives, remember?

NICKI: Whatever. You're not making any sense.

JOAN: OK. Bye.

NICKI: Close the door behind you.

(JOAN exits.)

TALK BACK!

1. Why do people take drugs? If you could give parents advice about how to prevent or stop drug use, what would you tell them?

2. Why do people cut themselves? What do you think a person like that seeks? What are they getting out of it? How might you be able to stop them?

3. Can you make someone go through rehab or does a person have to want to go?

4. How (if at all) should Dom be treated differently since rehab? How much should his parents trust him to stay clean?

5. What would be a better way for Nicki to make herself understood?

6. What should Nicki's friends do with this new, potentially life-threatening information about her?

ABOVE

1F, 6M

WHO

FEMALES
Wendy

MALES
Andrew
Elliot
Heath
Jasper
Joel
Ryan

WHERE Scene 1: A boarding school dorm room; Scene 2: A room in Jasper and Wendy's home.

WHEN Scene 1: Morning; Scene 2: Evening.

🎭 Andrew: You need to be as charming as possible, otherwise, no one would put up with you. Ryan: Make a decision about whether Wendy is right or wrong. You don't have to share that decision with anyone, but see if you can *subtly* hint at the truth earlier in the play.

✍ The monologues in Scene 1 are from my book *Teens Speak: Boys 16–18*. Find a monologue and build a scene around it, making the setting and characters more detailed and clear.

Scene 1: The Andrew Show

ANDREW: I am so sick. That was an excellent party, Graves. Seriously excellent. You really came through for us, buddy. Why didn't you tell us your sister is hot? And her friends . . . You are a lucky man, Graves. I'm not going to be able to walk for a week. I can't even remember getting home! Someone tell me what a great time I had!

HEATH: You were a total embarrassment.

ANDREW: No. Be serious.

HEATH: You were a puking mess.

ANDREW: No, man, be serious!

ELLIOT: You spent the night on the bathroom floor.

ANDREW: Don't mess with my head. It's not funny. Tell it like it happened.

JASPER: You spent the night on the bathroom floor with my dog.

ANDREW: I did not spend the night sleeping on the floor with your dog! No way! I remember a hot chick. A brunette bombshell.

JASPER: That was Trixie. My dog.

ANDREW: Stop it now. I mean it. No way did it go down like that. I hate you guys. You're full of it. Don't even talk to me.

ELLIOT: Fine. You asked and we told.

ANDREW: But you lied.

HEATH: You wish, my friend.

ANDREW: Shut up.

(JOEL and RYAN enter.)

JOEL: How was the party? I'm sorry I missed it.

ANDREW: Schwartz, you are truly lame. Getting the flu on a party night is pathetic and sad.

JOEL: It's not like I did it on purpose.

JASPER: You better now?

JOEL: A little.

RYAN: How about you, Andrew? I checked in on you when you were in Jasper's bathroom with Trixie and you were pretty bad off.

ANDREW: I'm fine, OK?

RYAN: OK. Just trying to be a friend. I mean, you were puking and crying into Trixie's fur for ages.

ANDREW: Very funny.

RYAN: Funny?

HEATH: He doesn't believe that happened. He thinks he spent the night with a babe.

RYAN: You do? You really shouldn't drink so much, Andrew. Seriously.

JASPER: You didn't make out with Trixie, did you?

ANDREW: No! Don't be disgusting! You guys are sick. So just shut up already. **Let's talk about something important and *factual* for a minute. About the history test. One cough means true, two means false. If A is the answer, press one finger to your temple like so. (Demonstrates.) B is two fingers to your temple and so on. To indicate we're moving on to the next question, stretch like you're yawning. We're always half asleep in Farber's class anyway. And, for God's sake, try to look casual. Like you're thinking. Last time you couldn't have been more obvious, Ryan. It's a miracle we weren't caught. We can't take that chance again. Once again, if I get an A average, in case anyone has forgotten, *I will get a new car of my choice.* That means beer runs, that means girls in the backseat. Get my drift? Do you need me to say it again? Now don't mess this up.**

JOEL: You can be really bossy, Andrew, you know that?

ANDREW: It's for your own good, Schwartz.

RYAN: Listen, I'm obviously not a very good faker, so maybe I should opt out of this. I don't want to get you guys in trouble.

ANDREW: McAvee! We are counting on you! Since Schwartz was sick yesterday, you're our next best hope!

RYAN: Be serious.

ANDREW: I am serious! Back me up here, people.

ELLIOT: You're smarter than us, Ryan. Without you and Joel, the rest of us would be C students.

JASPER: No lie. We're just idiots with money and you know it.

HEATH: You just need to stay calm and not panic, Ryan. Take it slow. No one yawns in a hurry. Just be calm.

ANDREW: Tell ya what. Why don't you guys go down to breakfast, and McAvee and I will go over the history test signals.

ELLIOT: Whatever.

JASPER: Works for me. Let's hurry before all the Fruit Loops are gone.

HEATH: Just stay calm, Ryan.

JOEL: Don't talk about Fruit Loops. I feel nauseous.

ANDREW: Go away before you puke on me, Schwartz.

(JOEL, HEATH, JASPER, and ELLIOT exit.)

ANDREW: OK, McAvee. You need to keep cool under pressure. We're all depending on you.

RYAN: That statement did not help.

ANDREW: You're too wound up! You need to take it easy. Want me to give you something for your nerves?

RYAN: No. That's OK.

ANDREW: Come on, McAvee, it would really help.

RYAN: No, no. I'm OK.

ANDREW: Listen to how you just said that. "No! No! I'm OK!" All panicked and scared. You need to chill.

RYAN: Look, I can't help it. This is my personality.

ANDREW: So take something. It'll help. You'll see.

RYAN: I'd rather not. I'm OK. Really.

ANDREW: *(Mocking.)* "I'm OK! Really!"

RYAN: I don't sound like that.

ANDREW: Sure you do, McAvee.

RYAN: How come you never call people by their first names?

ANDREW: Sure I do. What the hell does that have to do with anything?

RYAN: I just find it a little strange that you won't call people by their first names. It makes you sound like a gym teacher.

ANDREW: What the hell, McAvee? If you want me to call you Ryan, just say so.

RYAN: Call me Ryan.

ANDREW: Fine, Ryan. Now, about you being spasmodic . . .

RYAN: I'm not spasmodic. I'm perfectly fine.

ANDREW: Even Schwartz knows how to let loose from time to time. I'm not trying to corrupt you or anything, Ryan, I'm trying to help you. We're friends, right?

RYAN: Right.

ANDREW: So, I'd like you to have a day when you're relaxed for once.

RYAN: But I told you, I'm fine. This is just how I am.

ANDREW: Fine. Whatever you say. But if you mess this up for us, McAvee, you're dead.

RYAN: Ryan.

ANDREW: Ryan. Whatever.

RYAN: Well . . . I won't mess it up. Anyway, I don't plan to or anything.

ANDREW: Well, that's quite a relief. Excuse me if I'm not very convinced, Ryan.

RYAN: What do you want from me? How do we know

that if I take your pill I won't get . . . I don't know, maybe it will make me stupider or something. We don't know that.

ANDREW: Take the pill; don't take the pill. Doesn't matter to me. I just want my A average to last 'til I get my car and get into an Ivy League. That's all. And I am not going to let you mess that up for me, Ryan.

RYAN: As if I would. You talk like I'm trying to sabotage you or something.

ANDREW: I know you wouldn't do that. That's not what I mean. I know that you're a good guy. You're doing your best. But your best is a little dangerous for me right now, Ryan. Know what I mean? I can't afford any mistakes at this point. So you need to keep your head. You need to stay calm, cool, and collected. We're all in this together. You know that my success means your success, right?

RYAN: I guess.

ANDREW: Don't guess—know. Know it. I'll do whatever I can to make sure you're up there at the top with me, Ry.

RYAN: But you don't mean that, Andrew. You're looking out for number one.

ANDREW: Hey! That is really uncalled for! Seriously, Ryan. I can't believe you'd say that. We're all in this together.

RYAN: Come on, Andrew. You don't even think of me

as one of your best friends. We both know you're using me as your backup for Schwartz. He's your best friend, not me. I'm just the extra brain for when he get the flu and all that.

ANDREW: What are you talking about? God, you sound like a girl.

RYAN: Shut up, Andrew.

ANDREW: Ryan, I am just . . . It's not about who's whose best friend. We're not in third grade here. You're my friend, and when the time comes for us to share the spoils of our success, you'll be there. You're part of the group. I don't know where this Schwartz business is coming from.

RYAN: You told me last night I was a loser.

ANDREW: No, I didn't.

RYAN: You did. At the party. When you were with the dog in the bathroom.

ANDREW: First of all, I don't know what this dog business is about. It's not funny anymore. Second of all, I was clearly drunk, Ryan. One is not responsible for what one says when one is drunk.

RYAN: You were probably telling the truth for once, though.

ANDREW: Ryan, stop acting like a five-year-old. I was drunk and you're my friend. So let's just shut up about this. Let's go to breakfast and get me an A on this history test. Keep your eye on the prize, Ryan. I mean it. Are we cool?

RYAN: I guess so.

ANDREW: Don't guess so. Know it.

RYAN: Yeah, yeah.

ANDREW: Ry, you know if you have a problem you can come to me, right?

RYAN: I guess.

ANDREW: It's true. We're in this together. Let's go. If we hurry we might get some Frosted Flakes.

RYAN: Probably just Shredded Wheat is left.

ANDREW: I hate Shredded Wheat.

RYAN: Me, too.

ANDREW: You sure you don't want a little breakfast supplement?

RYAN: What? Oh, no. No. I don't do that stuff really.

ANDREW: You're a better man than me, Ry.

Scene 2: Low

WENDY: Hi.

RYAN: Oh, hi.

WENDY: What are you doing in here?

RYAN: I don't know. Should I not be here?

WENDY: No, no. It's fine. It's just that I was wondering since the party's in the other room . . .

RYAN: I guess I just wanted a break. To think.

WENDY: What are you thinking about?

RYAN: Nothing really.

WENDY: I'm Wendy, Jasper's sister.

RYAN: I know. I mean, I was here at the last party, too. I'm Ryan.

WENDY: I know. I saw you last time. It was really nice of you to try to help that really annoying guy at the last party.

RYAN: Who?

WENDY: Oh God, what's his name? The guy with the really big mouth.

RYAN: Oh, you mean Andrew?

WENDY: Yeah, that's him. The guy who was totally drunk.

RYAN: Yeah, well, we're friends.

WENDY: Oh. Sorry. You seem a lot different than him. Maybe when he's drunk he gets a little obnoxious.

RYAN: No, he's just like that.

(ANDREW enters.)

ANDREW: Where's my woman? Wendy! Wendy. Wendy, you ran away from me! Are you intimidated by my manliness? You wouldn't be the first one.

WENDY: No. I don't like you. No offense, Ryan.

ANDREW: Ryan? What are you doing in here with Ryan when you could be making out somewhere with me?

WENDY: Thanks for the offer, but . . .

ANDREW: But what? I promise I won't bite. Unless you want me to!

WENDY: You're talking really loud.

ANDREW: I want to make sure you hear me. Most girls like my voice.

WENDY: I guess I'm not most girls.

RYAN: Andrew, maybe you should sit down for a while.

ANDREW: Don't mind if I do.

(ANDREW sits down between WENDY and RYAN. WENDY is not happy about this.)

ANDREW: Isn't this cozy?

WENDY: Not really.

RYAN: Maybe you should rest for a while, Andrew. Take a break.

ANDREW: Maybe you're right. Maybe Wendy and I should have a quiet little moment. Curl up on the couch.

WENDY: I don't think so.

RYAN: If you want—

WENDY: Stay, Ryan! Please.

RYAN: OK.

ANDREW: Ryan, you're very safe, aren't you? You're a very safe person.

RYAN: What do you mean?

ANDREW: Well, McAvee, you make people feel nurtured. Like a mother. Isn't that right, Wendy?

WENDY: I wouldn't say that.

ANDREW: No, no! It's true. Ryan here has a motherly quality.

RYAN: Thanks a lot, Andrew.

ANDREW: I mean it as a compliment, Ryan. You're in touch with your womanly side.

RYAN: Shut up.

ANDREW: It's a good thing. Take the lovely Wendy here. It makes her feel safe and secure to have you in the room when I'm around. I, on the other hand, make her feel . . . what, Wendy? How would you describe it?

WENDY: Annoyed?

ANDREW: Insecure. Scared. In danger. Because I'm a manly, dangerous kind of guy.

WENDY: You wish.

RYAN: What are you trying to say, Andrew?

ANDREW: Nothing. That's all I'm trying to say. You're a nice person, Ryan. A very nice person.

WENDY: You say that like it's a bad thing. It's not. It's a good thing.

ANDREW: Right.

(ANDREW *puts his hand on* WENDY's *leg.*)

WENDY: Get your hand off of me.

ANDREW: Why?

WENDY: Because I said to. You know, you rich guys make me sick. You think you can have anything or anyone you want. Well, you can't.

ANDREW: Sure I can. I've always gotten everything I want. And not because I'm rich, though it doesn't hurt, it's because I'm charming. People like me, Wendy.

WENDY: Well, I don't like you. I think you're an obnoxious jerk.

ANDREW: Have you ever stopped to think that you get so angry with me because you're trying to fight your feelings for me? You're sexually frustrated, Wendy.

WENDY: You wish.

ANDREW: I know.

(ANDREW dives in for a kiss. WENDY puts her hand right on his face and pushes him away.)

WENDY: Go away!

RYAN: Maybe we should go back to the party, Andrew.

ANDREW: What is your problem? Are you some kind of prude?

WENDY: You're the one with the problem.

RYAN: Let's go back to the party, Andrew.

ANDREW: Man, you are one frigid, stuck-up bitch.

WENDY: If finding you repulsive makes me a frigid, stuck-up bitch then I guess that's what I am. Personally, I just think I'm intelligent.

ANDREW: You are one frigid, stuck-up bitch.

RYAN: Let's go back to the party, Andrew.

ANDREW: I'm going to go back to the party.

RYAN: Let's go.

ANDREW: I'm out of here, bitch. You just lost the opportunity of a lifetime.

(ANDREW exits. RYAN stands up to follow him.)

WENDY: No, Ryan. Just let him go.

RYAN: But he's drunk. He's going to get himself into trouble.

WENDY: What are you talking about? Did you even just see how he acted toward me?

RYAN: *(Sitting.)* Well, yeah.

WENDY: He was a jerk!

RYAN: Yeah. He was drunk.

WENDY: From what my brother says about him, he's always a jerk. Even when he's sober.

RYAN: Sometimes he's OK.

WENDY: Jasper says that Andrew is especially a jerk to you. He uses you. I mean, what he said about you just now is not the kind of thing you say to a friend. Especially one trying to help you out.

RYAN: He's an OK guy. Really. *(Beat.)* Lots of times he's really decent and generous.

WENDY: He's buying you. Just like he does with that other kid, Schwartz. But that kid doesn't seem to care. It bugs you, I can tell. So why do you let him say those things to you? Why don't you find another friend?

RYAN: Most of the time, Andrew is cool to me.

WENDY: You like him, don't you?

RYAN: Of course I like him. We're friends.

WENDY: That's not what I mean. I know you're so-called friends, but you *like* him, don't you, Ryan?

RYAN: No! Don't be stupid.

WENDY: I have never in my life been stupid. You like him. *(Beat.)* You know he doesn't like you back. He doesn't like you at all. Not even as a friend. He's a jerk, Ryan. I'm sorry to say so, but he is. And I'm not saying that to be mean because I like you—I guess you could tell that—I'm just saying it because it's true. But he's a horrible guy. Even if he was gay, you could do better. Anybody would be better. Believe me, part of me doesn't want to tell you this because I want you to . . . I don't know . . . somehow decide you like girls and me especially. But I guess that's not going to happen, and I hate to see a guy like you get treated like this. You deserve better.

RYAN: You really are crazy. You're not nearly as smart as you think you are. For starters, you don't understand guys at all. Andrew and I are *friends*. And guy friends aren't like girlfriends. We don't sit around talking about our feelings and all that crap. Sometimes we're competitive. Sometimes we're jerks. That's how guys are. I'm sorry to have to tell you that, but it's true. We're all pigs. And we don't think about people's feelings. And, besides, I am not gay. That's disgusting. I don't know where you get off—It's just not possible. I'm not like that. So you can just forget it. Just because I'm not into you doesn't mean I'm gay. You've got to be pretty full of yourself to think that. Maybe I'm just not attracted to you. Maybe I'm attracted to girls— lots of girls—but not to you. Ever consider that? Because that's the case here. I'm not going to hit on you because I don't like you, OK? So maybe you should consider things like that before you jump to conclusions.

WENDY: Come on, Ryan. I'm not going to tell anyone.

RYAN: Shut up, OK?

WENDY: Ryan, don't be like him. Andrew's a jerk and you're not—

RYAN: Maybe I am! I mean, I don't know, maybe you are a stuck-up bitch.

WENDY: Maybe I am. But I'm not stupid. And I'm not blind.

RYAN: Well, you're definitely crazy.

WENDY: You know I'm right.

RYAN: I know you're crazy.

(RYAN starts to exit.)

WENDY: Running off to him, McAvee?

RYAN: Just leaving, OK?

WENDY: Right.

(RYAN exits.)

WENDY: I'm sure. Boys are so stupid.

TALK BACK!

1. What do you think of Ryan? Is he a sucker? Is he gay?

2. What do you think of Andrew? Is he generous or selfish?

3. Is Wendy right or does she just wish she was right?

4. Every relationship has boundaries. What are some boundaries that, if crossed, would destroy a friendship for you?

5. Do you think bribing someone to help you is ethical? If the result is positive for both parties, is it still wrong?

6. If you could cheat your way through school, would you? Why or why not?

ODDS ARE

4F, 4M

WHO

FEMALES   MALES

   Cindy   Brad

   Jazmyn   Lon

   Kath   Diesel

   Lena   Sarc

WHERE   Scene 1: Outside; Scene 2: A café or food court.

WHEN   Present day.

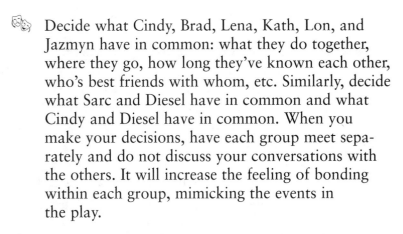 Decide what Cindy, Brad, Lena, Kath, Lon, and Jazmyn have in common: what they do together, where they go, how long they've known each other, who's best friends with whom, etc. Similarly, decide what Sarc and Diesel have in common and what Cindy and Diesel have in common. When you make your decisions, have each group meet separately and do not discuss your conversations with the others. It will increase the feeling of bonding within each group, mimicking the events in the play.

It's a classic dilemma: star-crossed lovers, like Romeo and Juliet. Write a scene or play taking place during the present day that explores this theme.

Scene 1: Even

(DIESEL accidentally bumps into CINDY with his guitar case. As a result, she drops her books.)

CINDY: Ow! Thanks a lot.

DIESEL: Sorry. I didn't mean to.

(DIESEL and CINDY collect CINDY's books.)

CINDY: Thanks.

DIESEL: Let me carry them. It's the least I can do. Then we'll be even.

CINDY: No, that's OK.

DIESEL: I don't mind. Where are you going?

CINDY: Um, I'm just going. I don't know where.

DIESEL: I was just trying to help. I didn't mean to scare you.

CINDY: You didn't scare me.

DIESEL: Yeah, I think I did. Cheerleaders tend to get a little jumpy around me.

CINDY: Well, I'm not. And I'm not a cheerleader.

DIESEL: You look like a cheerleader.

CINDY: And you look like . . .

DIESEL: Trouble?

CINDY: A musician.

DIESEL: I am a musician. A guitarist, as you can see.

CINDY: Oh. Well.

DIESEL: So I guess I didn't hurt you at least permanently, right?

CINDY: No, I'm fine.

DIESEL: So if you're not a cheerleader, what are you?

CINDY: I'm just a girl.

DIESEL: Do you play tennis?

CINDY: What?

DIESEL: What's with the short skirt?

CINDY: I go to Catholic school.

DIESEL: Oooh.

CINDY: What does that mean?

DIESEL: Nothing. It just means I get the skirt now.

CINDY: That wasn't what you meant. What did you mean?

DIESEL: You're feisty.

CINDY: Are you trying to scare me?

DIESEL: No.

CINDY: Well, then, just . . . whatever you're doing, just stop it.

DIESEL: I'm not doing anything.

CINDY: You're making assumptions. I can see it.

DIESEL: No, I pride myself in being a pretty open guy. People judge me a lot, so I try not to do the same. It bugs me. So it would be hypocritical for me to be like that. So I wasn't judging you. I was just observing and listening. That's all. You just seem a little jumpy, that's all. And I like to, when I can, sort of debunk people's opinion of me. So, if you're scared or intimidated by me, I'd like the opportunity to prove that I'm a decent person. That's all.

CINDY: Well, you picked up my books . . .

DIESEL: Right. And if there's any way I can make up for my clumsiness I'd kind of like to do it. You seem like you could be nice. Maybe we'd even get along. Who knows?

CINDY: Are you . . . Are you . . . trying to pick me up?

DIESEL: See? People always go for the most obvious thing. And no one really listens. I meant what I said. I'd like to make up for bumping into you. And I'd like to maybe get to know you better to see if we get along. It might be interesting, us having different backgrounds. That's not picking you up. That's not hitting on you. I'm just making a suggestion and being open to the universe. Maybe we bumped into each other for a reason.

CINDY: Like what?

DIESEL: Like maybe we're supposed to learn something from one another. Maybe I'm supposed to show you that guys who look tough or edgy or however you see me can really be nice and normal.

CINDY: Like I said, you don't scare me. And I'm not assuming anything. Here's what guys don't understand. It doesn't matter who the guy is or what he looks like. Girls always have to be on guard. I'd like to be like you and never have to worry about who's behind me or if anyone's following me, but that's just unrealistic for a girl. You have to be constantly on guard. You always have to assume the worst to keep yourself safe. So it's nothing personal. It's just how it is.

DIESEL: What do you think is going to happen?

CINDY: Guys are stronger than girls almost always. It's, unfortunately, a biological fact. So I could be mugged or kidnapped or raped—who knows? Maybe that sounds dumb or remote, but it's possible. And I, personally, don't want to take any chances. Better to be safe than sorry.

DIESEL: So are you always careful? Do you ever do anything daring and wild?

CINDY: Now, see, you did make assumptions about

me. Maybe you're not as open as you think. Just because I go to Catholic school doesn't mean I'm good and sweet and meek in every way. I'm a human being with lots of levels and complexity.

DIESEL: I can see that.

CINDY: You can't see that. It's invisible to the eye. I'd look schizophrenic if you saw in an instant how complex and varied I was.

DIESEL: Yeah, but everybody's like that, right? So why would you be any different?

CINDY: True. Exactly.

(Beat.)

DIESEL: This is a pretty good conversation, right?

CINDY: I guess.

DIESEL: Well, it is for me. I do think you're feisty. I like that. It's interesting.

CINDY: Well . . . thank you. And you seem intelligent.

DIESEL: I am. Do you know that no one in school, even my friends, really knows that? I don't tell anyone and they all assume I'm sort of average or worse. But I get mostly A's. That is, when the teachers aren't determined to see the worst in me.

CINDY: They're not allowed to do that. Their job is to be impartial.

DIESEL: Nice theory. Don't tell me you believe that. Haven't you ever noticed that the pretty girls get treated the best? Well, maybe not since . . .

CINDY: Since what?

DIESEL: I don't want to freak you out.

CINDY: What do you mean?

DIESEL: Well, I was going to say since you're pretty maybe you wouldn't notice that. But it's true. Then after the pretty girls, the really geeky guys get treated next best because the teachers assume they're the most intelligent. Another stereotype that's not necessarily true. Just because you wear glasses and have an asthma inhaler doesn't mean that you're a genius or anything.

CINDY: Well, of course not.

DIESEL: But that's what people think.

CINDY: But maybe people think those things for a reason. These stereotypes exist, I guess, because they often times are true.

DIESEL: That's a cop-out. Plus, you don't believe that. You got mad when I thought you were all repressed and snobby because you were a Catholic schoolgirl.

CINDY: Well, maybe . . . it's not entirely untrue. Of course, it's not entirely true, either. But people also don't get mad about things that don't have some grain of truth, unfortunately.

DIESEL: What about people wrongly accused of murder and stuff like that?

CINDY: Well, I guess in a case like that you would get mad over a lie.

DIESEL: But I see what you mean. If someone who's incredibly strong gets called a weakling, they're just going to laugh, right?

CINDY: Well, exactly.

DIESEL: Are you sure I can't carry your books anywhere? That sounds so old-fashioned, doesn't it?

CINDY: A little.

DIESEL: So, can I? I'm headed to Grant Street—that's where we rehearse. I could at least help you part of the way.

CINDY: That's OK.

DIESEL: Really?

CINDY: Really.

DIESEL: You sure?

CINDY: I'm sure! I'm fine!

DIESEL: You're not saying that because you still think I'll attack you or something, do you?

CINDY: No! I'm just fine on my own. Really!

DIESEL: OK, OK! Just checking. So if you're not freaked out by my appearance, how about you go out with me?

CINDY: So . . . I'm really confused.

DIESEL: OK, now I am sort of hitting on you. But in the nicest possible way. I like you.

CINDY: Well, thanks.

DIESEL: Hey, you don't know my name. It's Diesel. At least that's what my friends call me. My real name is really horrible. Don't even ask.

CINDY: OK. Hi, Diesel. I'm Cindy.

DIESEL: Hi, Cindy. Wow, our names don't exactly fight the stereotypes, do they?

CINDY: Not exactly.

DIESEL: So what do you say, Cindy? Maybe we could do something tomorrow?

CINDY: OK. Sounds good.

DIESEL: Great. Tomorrow.

CINDY: Should we meet here?

DIESEL: Sure.

CINDY: Nice meeting you, Diesel.

DIESEL: Likewise!

Scene 2: Odd

LENA: I cannot wait to meet this guy, Cindy.

CINDY: He is so great. You're going to love him.

KATH: I know we will.

CINDY: Remember, he looks a little different than the usual kind of guy we meet.

JAZMYN: So let's hear more about that. What does he look like?

CINDY: Well, he's kind of a rocker kind of guy. He's in a band.

KATH: That's so romantic!

LON: Why is that romantic?

KATH: All girls dream about dating a rock star.

LENA: Or a movie star.

JAZMYN: Or a professional athlete.

BRAD: Well, the joke's on you because you're all going to end up with accountants and computer programmers.

LENA: No, we're not!

JAZMYN: You wish.

BRAD: What do you mean I wish? I'm not going to be either of those things. I'm going to be a lawyer.

KATH: Even worse. Yuck.

LON: How about doctors? Don't chicks like doctors?

CINDY: Don't say chicks.

KATH: Yeah, that is really bad.

LON: So answer my question.

LENA: I don't know. Doctors?

JAZMYN: They make a lot of money.

KATH: But only if they can pay off all their school loans after going to medical school.

LENA: Plus they're never home, right? They're on call all the time.

BRAD: Only some. Not if you're a podiatrist or something.

JAZMYN: Whoa. I think I can speak for all womankind when I say a foot doctor is not sexy.

LENA: Well, he'd have to look like Brad Pitt, anyway. Then maybe he'd be sexy.

KATH: Anyway, you guys, we got completely off the subject. We were talking about Cindy and her new boyfriend.

LENA: Tell us more! Tell us more!

CINDY: Well—

(*DIESEL enters with SARC.*)

DIESEL: Cindy! Hi! Sorry I'm late. Sarc's car is giving him problems, as usual.

CINDY: Hi! Come sit next to me.

(*DIESEL sits next to CINDY. SARC puts his keys downs and sits between KATH and LENA, who both look very nervous.*)

DIESEL: Hi, everybody. This is Sarc. He's our drummer.

CINDY: Oh! Let me introduce everybody. Sarc and Diesel, these are my very best friends Lena, Kath, Jazmyn, Brad, and Lon.

DIESEL: Hey.

CINDY: So . . . can I even ask? Sarc?

DIESEL: It's short for sarcastic. Sarc is a rather sarcastic guy, aren't you?

SARC: Just a bit.

DIESEL: See? So . . . How's everyone doing?

JAZMYN: OK. How are you?

DIESEL: I am well, thank you. Do you all go to the same school?

CINDY: Yeah. I've known these guys forever.

DIESEL: That's great!

SARC: Yeah, really great.

DIESEL: Of course it's great. Why wouldn't it be great?

SARC: They know your secrets. They know too much.

DIESEL: Hey, that's a good question. Can a person know too much about you?

CINDY: I don't know. I mean, I think it's good to be honest and not lie about yourself, but does everyone you meet need to know that you peed yourself in assembly when you were five?

DIESEL: You did that?

CINDY: No! It was just an example.

SARC: Yeah, right.

CINDY: I swear! Am I lying, you guys?

LON: No. Brad was the one that did that.

BRAD: Thanks a lot.

DIESEL: You and Sarc are going to get along great!

SARC: I'm sure.

DIESEL: So would you guys want to come to one of our gigs? We have one next week, and you're all invited.

CINDY: Where is it?

DIESEL: It's at our friend's party. It's going to be wild.

KATH: I think I'm busy.

LENA: Our parents won't let us do stuff on a school night.

DIESEL: It's a Saturday.

LON: I'm having a party Saturday.

CINDY: You are?

LON: Yeah.

CINDY: Oh. Well, I don't know what I'll do!

DIESEL: That's OK; go to his party. There will be other gigs.

CINDY: You are so great.

SARC: Look, this is fun, but if I don't get home soon my mom will kill me.

DIESEL: Can you believe he has a mom? Sorry to run, you guys. Maybe we can meet up another time?

KATH: Um, sure.

SARC: Right. We'll get together all the time.

LENA: It was nice meeting you.

BRAD: Yeah. Too bad you have to go.

JAZMYN: Another time.

DIESEL: See you soon!

SARC: It's been an experience.

(DIESEL and SARC exit. SARC leaves his keys on the table. There's a beat of awkward silence.)

KATH: You really like him?

CINDY: Yeah. I really, really like him.

LENA: But . . . you're so different.

CINDY: Only on the outside. We're very similar, actually.

BRAD: Yeah, right.

CINDY: What?

LON: You're not similar, Cindy.

CINDY: How do you know?

JAZMYN: It's obvious, Cindy! We know you *really* well and we can tell!

CINDY: You're judging on appearances.

LENA: People decide on their outside appearance. It reflects what they're like inside.

CINDY: So if our appearances don't match, we don't match?

LON: Exactly!

CINDY: You guys are so wrong. I can't believe you'd be prejudiced like this.

KATH: We're not being prejudiced; we're looking after you. I can see how he could be nice, but getting along long term? Can you imagine if you actually went to his gig? *You'd* be the freak, Cindy. Everyone would be staring at you and *his* friends would be saying, "That girl's all wrong for you." You know it's true. It works both ways. Have your parents met him?

CINDY: No. Not yet.

KATH: And why is that? It's because you don't want your parents to meet him. Because you know they'd freak. No way can you bring that guy home to mom and dad. Can you see him taking you to the prom? Or you in the mosh pit at his concerts? You go out to dinner together and you'll wear a pink dress and he'll wear a black T-shirt with a skull on it. You don't match. You're from different worlds. It won't work. I'm not saying this to hurt you. I'm saying this because I'm your friend and I care about you. This is a disaster waiting to happen. Maybe you're having a little rebel moment, but that moment will pass, Cindy, and you'll wonder what the hell you're doing with this guy. Break up with him now before things go terribly wrong and he hurts you.

CINDY: Why would he do that? He wouldn't hurt me. He *likes* me. And I like him. Maybe we dress differently, but so what? We have great conversations. He's smart. He's funny. We talk about real things like politics and racism and books and—just everything! He's so interesting and he's so nice to me. You guys don't get it at all. I can't believe I never saw how empty-headed you are.

LON: Wait a second here. We're all very intelligent.

CINDY: If you were so intelligent you'd see how surface and shallow you're being. There's more to a relationship than listening to the same music and having all the same thoughts. That's why I'd never go out with one of you guys! We're too much the same. It would be boring.

BRAD: Thanks a whole lot.

LON: But it makes my point! We do think the same and have the same background. And I'm able to clearly see that you and this guy don't go together.

CINDY: We're not as similar as I thought, though, you guys and me. You're not my friends or you would give Diesel a chance. He's so great. You're really missing out by not seeing that. Not only are you missing out 'cause you won't know him, you're also missing out because . . . I'm not sure we can be friends anymore.

LENA: You don't mean that.

JAZMYN: Come on, Cindy!

KATH: We're only looking out for you.

BRAD: We're your friends. We've been your friends our whole life, practically.

LON: I think you should give *us* a chance and not shut us down so quickly.

CINDY: What a joke! You're total hypocrites.

(SARC enters.)

LON: At least we're not idiots or freaks like your new friends.

(SARC walks up to the table and picks up his keys.)

SARC: Nice.

(SARC exits.)

TALK BACK!

1. Do opposites attract? Why or why not? Is the relationship between Cindy and Diesel going to last?

2. Would you give someone who's very different (how they look, the crowd they associate with) a chance? Why or why not?

3. Lena says, "People decide on their outside appearance. It reflects what they're like inside." Do you think you can judge a book by its cover or not? How much does *your* outward appearance reflect who you are? What does it show about you?

4. Are Cindy's friends prejudiced or caring? Why?

5. Do you agree with Cindy's monologue in Scene 1, that girls need to be on guard at all times and guys can be more open and relaxed?

6. Why are some people attracted to forbidden love? Are you?

WHAT YOU DO

4F, 3M

WHO

FEMALES	MALES
Caris	Dave
Chelsea	Jake
Deb	Yaeger
Jitney	

WHERE Scene 1: A college cafeteria; Scene 2: A college dorm room.

WHEN Present day.

🎭 Identify and sympathize with your character's viewpoint, even if it is different from your own. Never judge your character negatively. Always try to understand. This avoids any obvious stereotyping and keeps the audience on its toes to see what comes next.

✎ For many people, college is the first time they really are on their own (without parental supervision). Some people tread carefully into this unknown territory, and some dive in headlong. Speculate on this transitional time, or if you're in college, write about your experiences.

Scene 1: Nothing

CARIS: I feel so much better.

DEB: Me, too.

(*JITNEY enters.*)

DEB: Hey, Jitney.

JITNEY: Hey.

DEB: Jitney, know what we just did?

JITNEY: No.

DEB: Caris and I ate four slices of pizza each and shared an order of fries in the student center.

JITNEY: Oh.

CARIS: It was completely disgusting.

JITNEY: That's a lot of food.

DEB: Yeah, so we flushed it.

JITNEY: OK.

CARIS: I feel so much better.

DEB: All the taste and none of the guilt.

JITNEY: Doesn't your body absorb stuff anyway?

CARIS: Does it?

DEB: No way. Not if you get rid of it fast enough.

JITNEY: But how long did it take you to sit and eat all that?

DEB: Not that long. Like, ten minutes.

CARIS: We scarfed it.

JITNEY: Then you didn't really enjoy it, did you?

DEB: Jitney, you can really be a buzz kill.

JITNEY: I'm just trying to help.

DEB: What would help is if you weren't a buzz kill.

JITNEY: Fine.

DEB: I feel great.

CARIS: Me, too.

DEB: Hey, want some of my ulcer meds? It really helps with the burning.

CARIS: Sure.

JITNEY: You're going to take her medicine?

CARIS: Yeah. Why not?

DEB: Buzz kill!

JITNEY: Because you don't know—

DEB: Buzz kill!

JITNEY: —what it's going to do to you.

DEB: Buzz kill!

CARIS: Why don't you let me worry about me, OK?

JITNEY: Fine.

(DEB gives CARIS a "pill" and a water bottle. CARIS swallows the "pill." Beat.)

CARIS: You think you're better than us, don't you?

JITNEY: What?

CARIS: You heard me. You think you know more and you're better.

JITNEY: No.

CARIS: Tell the truth.

JITNEY: Well, not about everything.

CARIS: But about some things.

JITNEY: I guess so.

DEB: Well, maybe we are stupid, but we're concerned about our appearance. It's normal. If I had great genes, I wouldn't do this. But I have to work to be thin.

CARIS: Do you care at all about how you look?

JITNEY: Well, yes. But I guess not as much as you.

CARIS: I bet you do, but you're too scared to do anything about it.

JITNEY: What would I be scared of?

CARIS: That your mom would disapprove of what you do. That a boy might want to kiss you.

DEB: Oooooo! Scary stuff! Have you ever been kissed, Jitney?

JITNEY: Sure.

DEB: By who?

JITNEY: None of your business.

DEB: Ooo. Getting defensive!

JITNEY: No, I'm not. It's just not your business.

CARIS: She's lying.

(Beat.)

CARIS: So what did you eat today, Jitney? At lunch?

JITNEY: Grilled cheese.

DEB: Whoa! Really fattening.

JITNEY: Whatever.

CARIS: You are what you eat, Jitney. You're white bread and a slab of cheese.

JITNEY: Thanks. So I guess you're a pile of trash.

DEB: Nice! Come on, girls. Let's play nice. See the thing is, Jitney, that you're not actually what you eat. You are what's in your stomach.

JITNEY: So you're nothing then.

DEB: No, we're a shot glass full of granola, bottled water, and some ulcer medication.

JITNEY: Well, that's much better.

CARIS: Why do you have to be so stuck-up?

JITNEY: I'm not.

DEB: Come on, Jitney, you are a little. You have to admit it. You're very judgmental.

JITNEY: Well, I don't mean to be.

DEB: Then maybe that's something you can work on. And maybe we'll work on improving our eating habits.

CARIS: You're so diplomatic, Deb.

DEB: I know!

JITNEY: The thing is, I just don't understand why you do it. You *are* absorbing at least a certain amount of the calories you take in. I don't think you can avoid that. So what's the point? When I puke, it makes me really upset. I can remember each and every place I threw up in elementary school like it was yesterday because it was an *event* and it was terrible and embarrassing. Why would you want to do that on purpose? It makes your breath smell and you have to take ulcer medication because you're bringing up bile, which has to burn, and your teeth are going to rot—I just don't get it.

CARIS: That's because you're ordinary. You're a book-worm. And that's OK with you.

JITNEY: Do you really think that I don't care at all about my appearance? Just because I don't take two hours to get ready to go to class or puke up my meals doesn't mean I don't care. A person can worry and feel insecure without wearing perfume and curling their hair twice a day. I just choose to be more natural. It's more my personality. But that doesn't mean that I don't have the same is-sues as you. We're not a different species.

DEB: So then you understand why we do it. We do it because—well, I can only speak for myself—I do it because I'm insecure and obsessed with being thin. I admit it. I'm not clueless about myself. And I've heard every negative side effect there is. I know I'm probably taking in some calories. The thing is, I've tried being anorexic, too, and I just can't do that all the time. Sometimes I break down and I just need to eat. So this is what I do. When I'm feeling stronger, I go back to not eating. And I feel like I'm in control. I feel like I'm pretty. I feel sort of proud of myself because of my self-control. It's probably the way you feel when you get a good grade or something. I know for a fact that people pay more attention to me when I'm thin. Because I feel better about myself. The bottom line is I can't feel happy just being natural. It's not how I was brought up. I'm a glamorous person. I like being like that. So I need to do what I need to do to make sure that my clothes and my appearance fit how I feel on the inside. I've been fat and I'm not going back.

JITNEY: But you're killing yourself.

DEB: I know that. But we all die. And this isn't going to kill me for a long, long time because I go back and forth between eating and not eating.

JITNEY: But it still affects you.

DEB: I know.

JITNEY: So why do you do it?

DEB: Because I have to. OK? That's the bottom line. I've been to therapy. I've heard everything. But I have to. It makes me happy. Live and let live, Jitney. If it makes me happy you should respect that.

CARIS: And not be so high and mighty about everything. You're not perfect.

JITNEY: I know. You probably think I'm fat.

CARIS: No comment.

DEB: It doesn't matter what anyone else thinks, Jitney. It matters what you think. And of course you're not fat.

JITNEY: Then how can you think *you* are?

CARIS: *(To JITNEY.)* Just drop it, fatty. *(To DEB.)* I don't know how you can stand talking to her. Let's just get ready for tonight. We're going to a party, Jitney. What are you doing?

JITNEY: Nothing. Homework.

CARIS: Sounds like fun!

DEB: You can come if you want.

CARIS: Deb!

JITNEY: No, thanks.

DEB: You should really try to be more social.

JITNEY: It's not exactly my thing.

DEB: Don't knock it 'til you've tried it!

Scene 2: Something

(There are two beds onstage. DAVE, JAKE, and YAEGER carry DEB onstage. DEB is crying and yelling. CHELSEA follows. JITNEY is lying in bed, not moving.)

YAEGER: What's she yelling for?

JAKE: She's just out of it.

DAVE: I think she had a lot of vodka shots.

DAVE: Yeah, well, we got her here now, so . . . I guess we should put her down on the bed or something.

CHELSEA: Guys, Dave, don't think worse of her for this. She's a really cool girl. She just drank too much.

JAKE: I'll say. She totally freaked out.

ZORA: I don't think she ate much earlier and she went running today . . . I think the drinking just hit her hard.

DEB: *(Spacey and groggy.)* I need to get out.

DAVE: No, you don't.

DEB: I need to get out!

DAVE: Relax, Deb. It's OK.

DEB: Dave?

DAVE: Yep, I'm here.

DEB: OK.

(DEB settles back down.)

JAKE: Dude, she is so into you.

YAEGER: Well, I guess our job here is done.

CHELSEA: Can we just leave her?

JAKE: What else are we supposed to do?

CHELSEA: I don't know.

(Beat.)

JAKE: We all look like morons standing here.

JITNEY: Could you guys keep it down?

YAEGER: Oh my God. I didn't know anyone else was
here.

JAKE: Yaeger, you jumped, like, ten feet into the air.

YAEGER: Did not.

JITNEY: What are all of you doing in here? This is my
room.

CHELSEA: Your roommate is sick.

JITNEY: Well, what's wrong with her this time?

CHELSEA: She had too much to drink. So you'll take
care of her, right?

JITNEY: Just go. I don't know any of you people.

CHELSEA: Will you look after her?

JITNEY: She can take care of herself.

DAVE: OK, guys. I'll look after her. You can go. We don't need a whole crowd here.

YAEGER: Fine with me. Bye.

JAKE: Let's go back to the party.

(YAEGER, JAKE, and CHELSEA exit. Beat.)

JITNEY: You should go, too.

DAVE: I'm just going to make sure she's OK.

JITNEY: She's not dead.

DAVE: No, but she's not exactly great either.

JITNEY: Well, it's her own fault.

DAVE: You're not very sympathetic, are you?

JITNEY: Why should I be? I just woke up to a bunch of strangers in my room and my roommate screaming. It's not exactly pleasant.

DAVE: Doesn't it matter to you that your roommate is sick?

JITNEY: It's not like she got the flu. She's drunk. She picked this.

DAVE: You are cold.

JITNEY: Maybe I am. But I think I have every right to be. You seem fairly normal, I guess, but what if you weren't? What if some nut fished Deb's key out of her pocket?

DAVE: So you think someone would come over here and attack you?

JITNEY: It's not impossible. These things happen.

DAVE: Aren't you being just a little dramatic?

JITNEY: No! Listen, she does stupid things like this all the time. And I'm sick of it. Sorry if I upset your delicate sensibilities, but that's how I feel.

DAVE: You are cold.

JITNEY: Please. You're Dave, aren't you?

DAVE: Yes.

JITNEY: Well, I know a little more about you than you think I do.

DAVE: Like what?

JITNEY: I know that Deb sat outside your room for four hours the other day waiting for you to show up.

DAVE: So?

JITNEY: So you stood her up, Mr. Nice Guy.

DAVE: I had something come up. I told Deb about it. She understood.

JITNEY: Come on. She makes no effort to hide that she's into you, and you take advantage of it all the time. You play games with her. One day you'll be really nice and attentive to her, and the next day you'll pretend you've never met her. You take what you want from her and toss her away whenever you feel like it. It's all about you and your needs. And you're enjoying it. I can tell.

DAVE: You don't know me. I happen to like Deb.

JITNEY: Admit it. You don't like her all the time. You don't like her when other girls are around. Girls you think are attractive.

DAVE: Look, what goes on between me and Deb is between me and Deb. It's none of your business.

JITNEY: You're mad because I'm right. You're a player. You're playing her and you know it. And I know it. So stop trying to pretend like I'm so terrible, that I'm such a bitch because I don't want to clean up her puke any more. At least I'm not hurting her on the inside. At least I have her best interests at heart.

DAVE: So having her best interests at heart means totally ignoring her when she could use a friend.

JITNEY: It means teaching her a lesson sometimes. It means not helping her destroy herself.

DAVE: There you go being dramatic again.

JITNEY: So you think having her best interests at heart means getting Deb drunk and messing around with her, then ignoring her and messing around with every other female who comes into your line of sight.

DAVE: That's not what I'm like.

JITNEY: That's not what you *think* you're like. Why don't you leave already?

DAVE: No.

JITNEY: What? Hoping to get lucky with her while she's passed out?

DAVE: Shut your mouth. You don't know me. I wouldn't do that.

(DEB wakes up.)

DEB: Dave?

DAVE: I'm right here, Deb.

DEB: Oh, good. Thanks, Dave. I knew you'd be here.

DAVE: I am here. Because I care about you.

JITNEY: Please.

DAVE: Why don't you go away? Deb and I are having a conversation.

JITNEY: I don't think so. This is my room.

DEB: Please, Jitney? Five minutes?

JITNEY: Deb—

DEB: Please. Five minutes.

JITNEY: Fine. Five minutes. But no more. I'm tired.

(*JITNEY walks to the exit.*)

JITNEY: You know, this is my room, too!

(*JITNEY exits.*)

DAVE: She's a real gem. You didn't do too well, roommate-wise, did you?

DEB: She's OK. She's just weird.

DAVE: She was going to let you lie here and puke on yourself.

DEB: I didn't puke on myself, did I, Dave?

DAVE: No.

DEB: (*Getting emotional.*) I'm sorry, Dave. I know I'm terrible. I'm a terrible person.

DAVE: No, you're not.

DEB: Do you like me, Dave?

DAVE: Sure, I like you, Deb. Don't you know that? Look, I'm here, aren't I? That proves you matter to me. Don't get upset, Deb. There's nothing to get upset about. Shhh. Calm down. You know, you're really something, Deb.

DEB: I am?

DAVE: Sure you are.

DEB: I embarrassed myself.

DAVE: You shouldn't be embarrassed. Everybody goes through this. Everybody drinks too much sometimes. And you know who your friends are when you're in a condition like this.

DEB: So we're friends?

DAVE: We're definitely friends, Deb.

DEB: I don't want to be your friend, Dave. I thought you really liked me.

DAVE: I do like you. I like you a lot.

DEB: Like more than friends?

DAVE: Definitely like more than friends. You know that. Haven't I shown you that? Listen, that thing the other day when I didn't show up—you know I didn't do that on purpose, right? You said you understood. I had something come up.

DEB: What came up, Dave? You never said.

DAVE: Stuff came up, Deb. Just important stuff. I can't really talk about it. I had a friend in trouble. Like you are right now. And I'm a good person, Deb. I can't let down a friend or someone I really care about.

DEB: You're a good person, Dave. I'm sorry.

DAVE: Don't be sorry. You just need to understand that when I let you down it's never on purpose. Because I care about you. I'm here for you, Deb.

DEB: Good. Will you stay tonight?

DAVE: I probably should get back to the party, if you're feeling OK.

DEB: I don't feel OK, Dave. I would feel a lot better if you were here.

DAVE: Well, I don't know . . . maybe . . .

(JITNEY enters suddenly.)

JITNEY: Get out. Get out now.

DAVE: Listen, you don't get to tell me what to do.

JITNEY: This is my room. I'll call the police. Get out now.

DAVE: Jeez, you're roommate is uptight, Deb.

JITNEY: Shut up and get out.

(JITNEY pushes DAVE out the door.)

DEB: Dave!

JITNEY: He's gone. Now lie face down so you don't choke on your puke and die.

DEB: Dave really likes me, Jitney. You were wrong.

JITNEY: Whatever.

DEB: You should see him when we're alone. He really likes me.

JITNEY: Right.

DEB: He cares about me.

JITNEY: You bet. Now go to sleep.

DEB: Do you think he'll talk to me tomorrow?

JITNEY: He should.

DEB: He will. He likes me. Everything's starting to go right for me, finally.

(DEB settles down to sleep.)

JITNEY: *(Addressed to DEB.)* Whatever you say, Deb.

TALK BACK!

1. What do you think of Jitney? Is she right or wrong? Do you like her or hate her?

2. What do you think of Deb? Is she right or wrong? Do you like her or hate her?

3. What do you think of Dave? Is he a nice guy or a jerk?

4. How would you react if you knew a friend had an eating disorder? Is it any of your business? Is there a way to help?

5. If your friend were in Deb's position in Scene 2, would you help her? How? Can you see Jitney viewpoint?

6. Does Dave sincerely like Deb? Where do you think he was when he stood up Deb?

7. Have you ever been made to feel like a loser for standing up for your beliefs? What happened? How did it make you feel? Have you ever done this to someone else? What was your motivation?

THE RIGHT THING

1F, 2M

WHO

    FEMALES   MALES

      Alana   Jordan

                        Ross

WHERE Outside.

WHEN Present day.

🎭 Ross and Alana: This is a life-or-death situation. It might help to have a real-life substitution for the other person so you feel the importance of this situation. Jordan: Underplay this character. Try to make it hard for Alana to refuse your offer.

✎ Either write about the aftermath of this play or write about a life-or-death decision.

Scene 1: Help

(ROSS is pacing, agitated.)

ALANA: What's wrong with you?

ROSS: Nothing, OK?

ALANA: Something's wrong.

ROSS: I said it's nothing, OK?

ALANA: OK, OK! Just that ever since you got off the phone, you've been pacing like crazy and yelling at me.

ROSS: I'm sorry. I just . . .

ALANA: Can I help?

ROSS: No.

ALANA: Are you sure? I will if I can.

ROSS: No. There's nothing—it's nothing.

ALANA: OK. If you're sure.

(Beat. ROSS suddenly hits his hand against the wall.)

ROSS: I'm just so . . . I'm trapped, Alana. I'm in big trouble.

ALANA: What is it, Ross? Just tell me. You're acting crazy.

ROSS: I can't. It's too much. I'm just . . .

(ALANA *walks over to* ROSS *and touches him on the shoulder.* ROSS *pushes her hand away.*)

ROSS: Don't, Alana!

ALANA: What? I don't get you. I'm trying to be nice.

ROSS: Nice isn't going to help me. Nothing is going to help me.

ALANA: Just stop this. You're acting crazy. You know I'd do anything for you, right?

ROSS: That's what you say.

ALANA: I mean it. I'd do anything for you.

ROSS: You don't really mean it. Nobody really means it.

ALANA: I do. Try me.

ROSS: No.

ALANA: Come on, Ross. I can't help until you tell me what's wrong.

ROSS: You don't know what you're asking.

ALANA: Just say it.

(Beat.)

ROSS: Fine. Fine! Remember, you asked. I'm in trouble, Alana. Big trouble. I've been running some things around town for a guy and now something's gone missing. It's just gone, Alana. And I don't know exactly what it is, but it's important, expensive stuff. I had something, and now it's gone. Stolen. And I'm the one responsible. I'm the one who's going to be blamed for it. And I'm in huge, huge trouble. Unless I come up with the money to pay for what I lost, I'm going to be killed. They're going to kill me, Alana. There's nothing I can do! There's no way I can get my hands on this kind of money. I'm so stupid! I'm so stupid! How could I—I just turned my head for a minute and now . . . I have two weeks to come up with the money. But I couldn't come up with it in a lifetime. They are going to kill me, Alana. This is no joke. I'm going to die. My mom is going to be so mad! I'm the only person she has in the world, and now I go and do something like this. I was just trying to make things better, to bring some money home. I don't know what to do!

ALANA: So this is drug stuff.

ROSS: I don't know. They never said, I never asked.

ALANA: But that's what it was.

ROSS: Probably.

ALANA: How do you know it's worth so much? Maybe they're lying.

ROSS: They're not lying, Alana. And it doesn't matter if they are. These are not people you argue with.

ALANA: So how much money are we talking about here?

ROSS: An impossible amount. More than I'll ever make in two weeks.

ALANA: How much?

ROSS: A hundred thousand dollars.

ALANA: Wow.

ROSS: See? I told you.

ALANA: You need to run away.

ROSS: Where am I going to go? They'll find me.

ALANA: No, they won't. It's a big country.

ROSS: But I'd have to leave my mother. How do I know that they won't hurt my mother?

ALANA: I guess you don't know.

ROSS: This is my problem, and I have to be the person to deal with the consequences.

ALANA: No way. We're going to figure out how to get this money.

ROSS: How?

ALANA: Who do you work for? We should talk to him. We should find out if there's a way of dealing with this. A payment plan or something. Maybe some kind of work you can do to make up for it.

ROSS: That's never going to work. They don't care about anything but their money.

ALANA: Wouldn't they rather get some money than kill you and get no money?

ROSS: No, Alana! You don't understand. That's not how this works. These people don't negotiate. They don't sit down at a desk and write up contracts and have business meetings. They get their payment in full or they get their payment in blood. There are no other choices.

ALANA: I find that hard to believe. I know that happens in the movies, but this is life.

ROSS: Believe me or don't—that's the reality of the situation. I've tried to think of other alternatives, believe me! I don't want to die. I'm completely freaked out about this. I'm thinking maybe I just want to kill myself so at least I know I won't be tortured!

ALANA: Stop it!

ROSS: There's no way out. I'm going to die and I'm still a kid. I never thought this would happen. I just wanted to make some money . . .

ALANA: Ross, call that guy. Let me talk to him.

ROSS: I'm not getting anyone else involved in this. You stay out of it, Alana. *(Suddenly.)* Why couldn't I just work at McDonald's? I had to make money fast and easy. I couldn't do it the hard way. You never think it's going to be you, though. You never think this could happen. I can't believe this is happening!

ALANA: Call him, Ross. I'll talk to him. If you're right about this, it can't get any worse. At least let me try to make things better.

ROSS: I'll rob a convenience store. That should get me some money.

ALANA: A hundred thousand dollars? I don't think so.

ROSS: I don't know anyone rich. Maybe rob a bank.

ALANA: You can't rob a bank! You'll get killed.

ROSS: What's the difference? At least I'll die trying.

ALANA: Stop it, Ross. Call the guy. Let me talk to him. We have to try that first, before you try something crazy.

ROSS: No, Alana, you don't get it!

(ALANA quickly grabs ROSS's phone.)

ROSS: Give that to me!

(ALANA presses a few buttons on the phone.)

ALANA: I'm going to dial back the last number.

ROSS: Don't! Come on! Give it to me!

(ROSS *tries to grab the phone from ALANA. With difficulty, she manages to hold into it. They continue to struggle as she speaks on the phone.*)

ALANA: Yes. Hi. This is Alana, Ross's girlfriend. Hi. I wonder if we could talk about what happened. If we could work something out. Can we meet? Please? Beecher at the gas station? OK. Thanks—

(ROSS *gets the phone from ALANA and puts it in his pocket.*)

ALANA: You're too late. We're meeting. He seemed OK.

ROSS: Don't do it, Alana.

ALANA: Who knows? Maybe we can work something out, Ross. We have to try.

ROSS: I don't want to drag you into this! It's my own stupid fault.

ALANA: Maybe we can work something out, Ross. It's worth trying.

ROSS: This is only going to turn out bad. It's not worth it, Alana. I'm just going to—I don't know—I'm going to shoot myself or something. It's the only answer. There's nothing else to do.

ALANA: Stop talking like that! I said I'd do anything for you and I meant it. I'm going to help you with this, Ross. We're going to work this out. You're not going to die. I promise! Now just relax for a little while. The guy is coming to talk to us. What's his name anyway?

ROSS: Jordan.

ALANA: That's a reasonable name. Everything's going to be OK, Ross. I know it.

Scene 2: Anything

JORDAN: So. What can I do for you?

ROSS: Nothing.

ALANA: We don't know. I guess the real question is what can we do for you?

JORDAN: What do you mean?

ALANA: Ross doesn't have a hundred thousand dollars.

JORDAN: I'm not surprised.

ALANA: So we're just wondering—

ROSS: *You're* just wondering—

ALANA: *I'm* just wondering if there's anything else that he can do for you to make it up. It was an accident.

JORDAN: It was a very expensive accident.

ALANA: He didn't know it was so expensive. He didn't know what he was carrying.

JORDAN: He didn't? I don't see how that could be.

ALANA: What?

ROSS: Leave it alone, Alana. It doesn't matter anymore.

JORDAN: **Ross knew exactly what he was into. Maybe he kept that part from you so he would look more . . . sympathetic.**

ALANA: Ross, did you know?

ROSS: Well, I didn't know exactly . . .

JORDAN: But you knew it was drugs, Ross. Don't try to pretend you didn't. And I told you many, many times how important it was for you to keep your eye on your package. To be careful. That there was a lot of money on the line. And every time, you nodded. You said to me, "I get it, Jordan. I understand you." So now you're saying you didn't know? You didn't understand?

ROSS: I do. I did. I know.

JORDAN: So you see, that's that. Ross knew the consequences, and he was sloppy anyway. What's going on now is all Ross's fault, isn't it?

ROSS: Yes. I know. I didn't call you. She did.

JORDAN: Yes, she did. That's impressive, Ross. You've got a pretty girlfriend who'd face a notorious drug dealer for you. Pretty brave. Of her, I mean. You're obviously a coward and a stupid one, too.

ALANA: No, he's not.

JORDAN: See what I mean? You proved my point. You have more courage in your little finger than Ross here has in his whole body.

ALANA: That's not true.

ROSS: Don't speak for me, Alana! I can handle this myself.

ALANA: Your answer is to kill yourself. That's a great solution. How is that helping anyone?

JORDAN: Ross, life is precious. You're not even going to try to get us the money you owe? That doesn't reflect very well on you. It shows bad faith on your part.

ROSS: I don't have that kind of money. No one I know has that kind of money. Except for you.

JORDAN: Except for me.

ALANA: There must be some way we can work this out.

JORDAN: Tell you what. Ross, why don't you disappear for a while? So I can talk to your girlfriend here.

ROSS: Why?

JORDAN: Your girlfriend—What was your name again?

ALANA: Alana.

JORDAN: Alana and I are going to see if we can work something out.

ROSS: Well, I don't think that's a good idea.

JORDAN: I thought you wanted to work something out.

ROSS: Right, but—

JORDAN: So Alana and I are going to talk things through.

ALANA: It's OK, Ross.

JORDAN: Go on now, Ross.

(ROSS exits.)

JORDAN: Alana.

ALANA: Yes?

JORDAN: What do you have to offer me in exchange for a hundred thousand dollars?

ALANA: Well, I've been thinking about this, and I thought Ross could maybe work off the money. Like he could work for you without getting paid until you get your money back.

JORDAN: Nice idea, but not good enough. It will take a long time for him to make that kind of money.

ALANA: Well, even if he stole some money, it wouldn't be enough. That's a lot of money to come up with.

JORDAN: I know. That's why he should have been more careful.

ALANA: I know. But isn't there anything he can do?

JORDAN: You're very brave to talk to me like this.

ALANA: Well, thanks. But it's just talking. It's no
big deal.

JORDAN: Don't sell yourself short. Most girls would be
too scared to talk to a guy like me. Especially with
their boyfriends being scared, as he should be. What
did Ross tell you about me?

ALANA: Ross said you were going to kill him if he
didn't come up with the money. That's about all
he said.

JORDAN: Ross doesn't keep a very cool head, does he?

ALANA: Well, no. He's a little panicked. Worried.
Which I can understand. He's just a regular kid,
and he got in over his head. He was trying to
help out his mother. It's just him and his mom,
and she's been sick. So he wanted to make some
money to help out. You can understand that,
right? So I was thinking. I was telling Ross that
I thought you'd probably rather have at least
some of the money he owes you rather than none
of the money. And if you killed him you'd get
nothing. That makes sense to me. You get no
money from him if he's dead, right?

JORDAN: That's true. But then he'd be a warning for
anyone else who thought about being sloppy or
stealing from me.

ALANA: So you'd really just kill him?

JORDAN: I don't want to kill anyone.

ALANA: So just don't. **Let him pay it off in stages or something.**

JORDAN: I don't think I can do that.

ALANA: **There has to be something we can do!**

JORDAN: Well, I'm not unreasonable. We might be able to think of something.

ALANA: Good. What do you want? What can we do?

JORDAN: You really love your boyfriend, don't you?

ALANA: Sure I do.

JORDAN: Well, maybe you can help him.

ALANA: How?

JORDAN: Are you willing to help him?

ALANA: I don't want him to die.

JORDAN: He could die.

ALANA: So what can I do to help? Do you want me to deliver stuff, too?

JORDAN: Not exactly.

ALANA: What then?

JORDAN: What would you be willing to do?

ALANA: I'm a good worker. I could do whatever you wanted.

JORDAN: So you're up for anything?

ALANA: Well, sure. I guess.

JORDAN: Anything? To save your boyfriend's pathetic life?

ALANA: He's not pathetic.

JORDAN: Answer the question. Do you want to save his life? Are you willing to do anything? Or would you rather see him die?

ALANA: I don't want him to die. I'd do anything.

JORDAN: Because I really have no problem killing him. He's nothing to me.

ALANA: Don't. Please.

JORDAN: Here's what I'm thinking, Alana. You come and live with me at my house for a while.

ALANA: At your house?

JORDAN: Right. I feed you, give you a roof over your head . . .

ALANA: But what about my parents?

JORDAN: You'll think of something to tell them.

ALANA: So . . . what's in it for you?

JORDAN: Come on, Alana. You're a sensible girl. Do you really need me to spell it out?

ALANA: I'm not sure.

JORDAN: Come to my house. I'll take good care of you. I'll have some friends over. And if you're good, we'll let your boyfriend off the hook. He'll walk away alive, and you can have a happy life together. *(Beat.)* Or I could just kill him now. It's up to you.

(Beat.)

ALANA: For how long?

JORDAN: Oh, I don't know. A week or two. Or three.

ALANA: I have to go to school.

JORDAN: No school. I'm living proof that you don't have to go to school. You stay at my house. We're talking about a hundred thousand dollars, Alana. I think I'm letting you off pretty easily. It's your choice. Come stay with me for a while or watch your boyfriend bleed to death. What's it going to be?

TALK BACK!

1. Would you try to reason with Jordan? Why or why not?

2. If you were Alana, would you agree to Jordan's proposition to save Ross's life? Why or why not?

3. It's hard to imagine, but how do you think you'd react in Ross's situation?

4. Can you think of any other options for Ross and Alana?

5. How far would you go to support your family?

6. If someone offered you a way to make easy money, would you take it or walk away? Are you suspicious or trusting by nature?

7. How important are money and material things to you? Would you go outside the law to get what you want? Is there anything that would tempt you to break the law if you're normally a law-abiding person?

MERCY

4F, 4M

WHO

FEMALES	MALES
Beth	Joe
Laura	Mark
Natalie	Kurtis
Sara	Martin

WHERE Scene 1: The church basement; Scene 2: Kurtis's room.

WHEN Present day.

Scene 1 and Scene 2 should have two completely different energies. Scene 1 needs to build to fever pitch and have a sense of momentum. Scene 2 needs to be quieter, more reflective and personal.

Scene 1: You wake up tomorrow and you are yourself, but everyone around you is different. They are nothing like you. But you are told they're your friends. What do you do? Scene 2: You wake up tomorrow and you're exactly the opposite of how you are today. Get inside this new mindset. Try to see how some of your opinions and preferences can be seen as crazy to other people.

Scene 1: Wake

BETH: Kurtis, I'm so glad to have you back with us.

NATALIE: We missed you so much.

JOE: Yeah, man, things weren't the same without you.

KURTIS: Thanks.

LAURA: We should get the whole church group together and go out for pizza!

MARTIN: You could all come over to my house. I'm sure my parents wouldn't mind us having a party there. We could eat and read some passages—

KURTIS: Passages?

MARK: The Bible. You know.

KURTIS: Oh. Well. I think I might go home.

MARTIN: What?

SARA: Come on! It'll be fun!

KURTIS: Yeah, but we did that Bible thing yesterday.

JOE: Dude, we do it every day.

KURTIS: We do?

LAURA: Absolutely.

MARK: Yeah. We just like to hang out and share our

problems with people who understand and support our beliefs.

KURTIS: I guess that's a good thing. I just don't feel like it today.

NATALIE: You guys, maybe he's tired. He's been through a lot.

LAURA: We don't want to force you, Kurtis. You don't *have* to hang out with us.

KURTIS: No, it's not that exactly. It's just that everything is so new to me. I don't remember any of this. I don't remember any of you. It's all gone. I know we were friends before I got hurt, but, you know, poof! All that information disappeared. It's just so weird to have other people tell you who you are and what you like. How come *I* don't know what I like? Shouldn't I know?

SARA: Don't worry, Kurtis. It will all come back to you.

KURTIS: What if it doesn't?

MARTIN: What do you mean?

KURTIS: OK. Well, you said that we can all hang out and share our problems, right?

JOE: Right.

KURTIS: Can I be completely honest?

MARK: Of course. You should.

KURTIS: I don't know how into all this Bible stuff I am. It doesn't feel like me somehow.

BETH: But it is you. It's always been you.

LAURA: You were, like, the leader almost.

MARTIN: Listen, Kurtis, we've known you forever. Trust us.

KURTIS: Well, I do trust you. I just wonder if I'm a different person now. I'm just not having fun.

NATALIE: Don't worry about it, Kurtis. Everything's going to be OK.

KURTIS: Thanks, Natalie. But I feel fine, actually.

NATALIE: You don't hate us though, do you?

KURTIS: No, no! That's not it at all. I just am not . . . I don't know. I'm just not enjoying the things I guess I enjoyed before. Does that make any sense?

NATALIE: Sure it does.

MARTIN: Kurtis, if we're being honest—and that's something I believe strongly in—I have to tell you that you seem different. I think that coma did something to you. You're a different person. You used to be so passionate about your faith, and now . . . I'm worried about you.

KURTIS: I'm fine, Martin.

MARTIN: It's not just you I'm worried about. You're corrupting Natalie as well.

KURTIS: I'm not corrupting anyone.

NATALIE: What are you talking about?

MARTIN: Are you two fornicating?

KURTIS: Excuse me?

MARTIN: You heard me.

KURTIS: Did you just say "fornicating"?

MARTIN: You heard me, Martin.

NATALIE: We're not doing anything.

MARTIN: That's not what it looks like. You're throwing yourself at him. It's embarrassing to watch.

NATALIE: No, I'm not.

MARTIN: He's corrupting you. He's leading you to hell.

KURTIS: I'm not leading anyone to hell. I may be separating myself from the church group, but it doesn't make me a bad person. I'm just trying to work out who I am. I think I'm a decent, kind, good person. I'm sure I am. Not wanting to sing songs and read from the Bible all the time doesn't make me a bad person. I'm sorry to say it, but I find those Bible get-togethers really dull. I really want to look into other things. Like I think I'd like to get a pilot's license.

MARK: Who wouldn't?

MARTIN: While you were sleeping, Satan entered your soul, Kurtis.

BETH: He's just trying to work things out. He'll come back to us. After all, we're his best friends!

KURTIS: I still believe in God. I'm pretty sure. That's not different.

MARTIN: God doesn't want you going off in the middle of the night with Natalie.

KURTIS: What? I don't know where this is coming from. You've got it all wrong about Natalie and me. We're friends. That's all. Not that it's any of your business. Actually, I don't think God would approve of you walking around telling lies about people, Martin. Have you always been this much into the church thing? Was I? I can't imagine that I'd ever say "fornicating"! That's seriously bizarre. That's part of why I don't feel comfortable around you guys now. You're a little too into this stuff. This just isn't me. At least not anymore.

MARTIN: Is it "bizarre" to have faith then? Is it bizarre to have beliefs and morals? Is it bizarre to try to save your friend from the hand of the devil? I don't think so.

KURTIS: I'm not in any danger. I'm not evil. I'm just a little different from you. Just because I don't think like you or do everything you say doesn't mean I'm the devil.

MARTIN: I'm not asking you to do everything I say. But you're not acting like yourself. You're a different person. If that's not the work of an evil force, I don't know what is.

SARA: Um, guys, we're supposed to be having fun.

MARTIN: This isn't about fun. This is about saving Kurtis's soul.

KURTIS: Stop it.

JOE: Let's just have some pizza.

(MARTIN drops to his knees.)

MARTIN: Almighty God, please save Kurtis from himself. Help him find the strength to say no to evil. Help him say no to the sin of fornication. He needs help, Lord.

KURTIS: *You* need help! Just stop it.

MARTIN: Do you see how Satan possesses him? He used to be good, Lord. Take pity on him. He used to be one of your children. Now he's a fornicator, a coward, and a liar.

KURTIS: That's a very kind and loving thing to say, Martin.

MARTIN: I speak the truth. I speak the Lord's word. And I seek to redeem your soul. Your soul is on the line. Do you want to go to heaven and be embraced by the angels or be tormented eternally in hell? The choice is simple, Kurtis.

KURTIS: All because I didn't want pizza.

MARTIN: All because you have given over to sin.

NATALIE: He's right, Kurtis.

KURTIS: No, he's not.

NATALIE: Yes, he is.

KURTIS: But we didn't do anything.

MARTIN: Pray with me, Natalie. Pray for your soul and Kurtis's.

(NATALIE kneels and begins to pray silently. SARA kneels and does the same.)

MARTIN: We should all pray.

KURTIS: You know what I think? I think maybe you're just mad because you'd like to fornicate with Natalie!

NATALIE: Stop it!

LAURA: You're scaring me, Kurtis.

MARTIN: Pray with us!

(LAURA kneels.)

JOE: I guess it can't hurt.

(JOE kneels. BETH and MARK kneel. They all pray quietly.)

KURTIS: This is freaky. I think you're all nuts.

MARTIN: So that's what you believe? God is nuts?

KURTIS: I give up. I don't get this at all. I'm out of here.

MARTIN: We'll be praying for you.

(KURTIS exits.)

Scene 2: Waves

NATALIE: You were right, Kurtis. This church stuff—we've gone too far. It's too much.

KURTIS: Listen, you don't have to think what I think.

NATALIE: No, but I agree with you. I guess I'm just . . . scared a little.

KURTIS: Scared of what?

NATALIE: I don't know. It's just that Martin, Sara, and all of them are like my family. The church is like my family. And my family itself, well, they have a strong faith, too.

KURTIS: There's nothing wrong with that.

NATALIE: But lately things have been so serious. It used to be fun, you know? We'd go camping or have a party or whatever. It was about just getting together and having fun. But now . . . there's all this finger-pointing. And it's so . . . black and white. If you don't agree with Martin, just like you said the other day, if you don't agree with Martin then you're satanic or something. It's not right. I think . . . I think he thinks he's God or something. And until you came out of your coma, I guess I just didn't question things. Because no one else was. But what you said makes sense to me. Does it make me a bad person to say these things?

KURTIS: Like I said, you don't have to agree with me.

I don't want to be like Martin. I want to be more open-minded.

NATALIE: So what exactly happened to you in the hospital?

KURTIS: I don't know. I don't even remember the accident. It's all blank. All I can remember is waking up in the hospital and being told it was three months later. And all I could think of was, "How am I going to make up all that schoolwork?" Funny how the school looks past this stuff when they want to.

NATALIE: Well, they had to.

KURTIS: I'm not going to argue with them. Works for me. Anyhow, so I wake up but I can't remember my past. Only little bits, not enough to make sense of things. Like I'll remember that I had an ice cream cake for my fifth birthday and it melted in the sun and that someone at the party swallowed a bee.

NATALIE: That was Beth.

KURTIS: See? So I'll remember meaningless things, but not the big stuff. And then I'm being told here are your friends, this is what you believe, this is what you like to do—but nothing's adding up. I mean, I don't hate any of you guys, but I just don't feel the connection anymore. Because the history we had has been forgotten. And my beliefs seem different. My dad told me the other day that I love pickles, so I tried one. I hate pickles. They're nasty.

NATALIE: So do you hate religion and church now?

KURTIS: Not hate. That's too strong a word. It just doesn't interest me very much.

NATALIE: So what does interest you?

KURTIS: I don't know. That's the worst part. I honestly don't know. That's what I have to figure out.

NATALIE: Maybe I can help.

KURTIS: Listen, I don't want to put you at war with your friends. I know I'm not their favorite person at the moment. I don't want you to lose everything because I lost my memory. This is my problem, not yours.

NATALIE: But . . . I think I might be feeling the same things. I'm not sure. But then sometimes I feel like I shouldn't doubt or question. Because that's part of what was wrong with Thomas.

KURTIS: Thomas?

NATALIE: Doubting Thomas? In the Bible? He questioned Jesus.

KURTIS: And I guess that wasn't good.

NATALIE: Well, nothing really happened to him, but he was sort of, um, chastised for being like that. You're just supposed to believe. That's what faith is.

KURTIS: Well, I'm definitely no expert on anything right now, but isn't there a difference between having faith and doing whatever anybody tells you?

NATALIE: You really are different.

KURTIS: I've been afraid to ask . . . What was I like before?

NATALIE: You were very . . . sure of yourself. Confident. Kind of a leader. And kind of like Martin is now. But Martin struggles more with it. He tries to force it, and it came easily to you. I think he's . . .

KURTIS: Jealous?

NATALIE: Well . . . yeah.

KURTIS: Jealous of a guy who spent three months in a coma. That makes a lot of sense.

NATALIE: You are what he's not.

KURTIS: What's that?

NATALIE: Well, naturally sort of charismatic. People like you. People listen to you. And . . . I don't know.

KURTIS: He likes you, doesn't he?

NATALIE: I don't know. Maybe.

KURTIS: You say "I don't know" a lot.

NATALIE: I mean, I guess he does.

KURTIS: So, I guess you don't like him like that.

NATALIE: We're friends. We were a little closer when you got into the accident for a little while . . . We were all so worried about you. But I never really liked him like that.

KURTIS: But you maybe like me like that?

NATALIE: I don't know. I mean, you don't even know who you are. How am I supposed to know if I like you?

KURTIS: Good point.

NATALIE: But one thing is still the same about you.

KURTIS: What's that?

NATALIE: You've still got that quality about you that makes people want to be around you. I don't know what to call it . . .

KURTIS: Well, thanks. Obviously, people like to be around you, too.

NATALIE: I don't know about that.

KURTIS: Well, there's Martin and Sara and all that crew, and me.

NATALIE: Thanks.

KURTIS: So, something's still bugging me.

NATALIE: What?

KURTIS: When Martin got all crazy about me corrupting you and being the devil and all that business, you ended up agreeing with him.

NATALIE: Oh.

KURTIS: What was that about? We aren't so-called "fornicating."

NATALIE: Well . . .

KURTIS: Come on. My memory is not that bad. I remember everything that's happened since I woke up and I'm positive—Wait. Did it happen before the accident? Us?

NATALIE: Well . . .

KURTIS: I'm sorry I didn't remember.

NATALIE: You lost your memory, Kurtis.

KURTIS: I know, but . . . I must seem like a real jerk to you.

NATALIE: No. You just don't remember. It's OK.

KURTIS: So that's . . . Is that why you came to see me? To see if I remembered?

NATALIE: Well, partly.

KURTIS: Oh.

NATALIE: Also partly to work out how I'm feeling about . . . everything really.

KURTIS: Oh. I'm really sorry. So . . . was I . . . how could I be . . . I'm confused. So I was this super religious guy, right? How could I . . . ? I mean, was I just a jerk? Or a hypocrite?

NATALIE: I don't know. I know what you said to me when we were . . . close, but . . .

KURTIS: But what?

NATALIE: To be honest, I was never sure if I should believe it or if I just wanted to believe it. Not that you were a bad guy or anything. You were just always so convincing. Whatever you thought always seemed right. So when you said that you really loved me and that we would get married anyway . . . it didn't seem like such a big deal. So I . . . believed you. I guess . . . I loved you. So it didn't seem so bad, the two of us. The way you talked about it, it just made sense. And I felt like I'd be a fool to let it—to let you slip past me. I felt like the luckiest girl in the world. You liked me. You loved me. Everyone wanted to be near you, and you chose me . . . Then you got into the accident . . . I guess I just didn't know— don't know where we stand exactly. Where we are. How I'm supposed to feel. We were . . . you were everything to me and now . . .

KURTIS: I'm sorry, Natalie.

(Beat.)

KURTIS: I just don't know what to say. I don't remember any of this. So . . . How can I say this? I don't know if I can honor what I said before—

NATALIE: I know. It's OK.

KURTIS: I really don't know if I like who I was. I really want to do better this time around.

NATALIE: And that means being less religious?

KURTIS: It's weird, isn't it? Kind of funny. But that is one of the things I want to change. I think I want to experience things more before I believe. I guess I'm a doubter now.

NATALIE: There are worse things, I guess. You could be a murderer.

KURTIS: I hope not! Like I said, I don't want to make things worse for you. But I'd really like to still have you as a friend if you think that could work.

NATALIE: I don't know.

KURTIS: I thought that's what you wanted.

NATALIE: I don't know. I mean, part of me wants to, but the other part . . .

KURTIS: Sure.

NATALIE: **I guess I'm a little hurt. And confused. I almost wish *I'd* lose my memories.** Knowing the past makes things more confusing.

KURTIS: I don't know about that.

NATALIE: Well, you have an excuse to start fresh.

KURTIS: That's a good way to think of it. I think I'll use that.

NATALIE: Go ahead.

KURTIS: So you're going to go on doing the same thing?

NATALIE: It's what I know.

KURTIS: Don't you ever want to be rebellious? To do something dangerous?

NATALIE: I'm not as brave as you are. I thought maybe . . . But I don't think it's me.

KURTIS: It's a free country.

NATALIE: Yeah. I guess I'll go now.

KURTIS: OK.

NATALIE: Oh. One thing. You never liked pickles. That was your brother.

KURTIS: Are you serious? I feel so much better now. I guess I'm not the only one with memory loss problems.

NATALIE: Guess not. Bye.

KURTIS: Bye.

(NATALIE exits.)

TALK BACK!

1. What do you think of Martin? Is he a good guy or a bad guy or somewhere in between?

2. Are you a leader or a follower?

3. Do you have faith or are you a doubter? Which do you think is the better way to be?

4. What would you do in Natalie's situation? Are you more likely to continue on a path that's comfortable and familiar or to dare to try a new way of thinking?

5. Do you believe in God? Do you think Martin is trying to be God or do you think he's just acting on his faith?

6. Do you think Kurtis cared about Natalie before his accident? Is he corrupting her or just showing her a different way of thinking?

7. Is there a difference between being a good person and being a virtuous person? Explain your answer. Who in this play is good and who is virtuous?

APPENDIX

CHARACTER QUESTIONNAIRE FOR ACTORS

Fill in the following questionnaire as if you are your character. Make up anything you don't know.

PART 1: The Facts

NAME:

AGE/BIRTHDATE:

HEIGHT:

WEIGHT:

HAIR COLOR:

EYE COLOR:

CITY/STATE/COUNTRY YOU LIVE IN:

GRADE*:

BROTHERS/SISTERS:

PARENTS:

UPBRINGING (strict, indifferent, permissive, etc.):

* If you are an adult, what educational level did you reach (college, medical school, high school, etc.)?

PART 2: Rate Yourself

On a scale of 1 to 10 (circle one: 10 = great, 1 = bad), rate your:

APPEARANCE	1 2 3 4 5 6 7 8 9 10
IQ	1 2 3 4 5 6 7 8 9 10
SENSE OF HUMOR	1 2 3 4 5 6 7 8 9 10
ATHLETICISM	1 2 3 4 5 6 7 8 9 10
ENTHUSIASM	1 2 3 4 5 6 7 8 9 10
CONFIDENCE	1 2 3 4 5 6 7 8 9 10
DETERMINATION	1 2 3 4 5 6 7 8 9 10
FRIENDLINESS	1 2 3 4 5 6 7 8 9 10
ARTISTICNESS	1 2 3 4 5 6 7 8 9 10

Do you like yourself?	YES	NO
Do you like your family?	YES	NO
Do you like the opposite sex?	YES	NO
Do you like most people you meet?	YES	NO

Which of the following are important to you and which are not? Circle one.

WEALTH	Important	Not Important
KNOWLEDGE	Important	Not Important
POWER	Important	Not Important
PEACE	Important	Not Important
POPULARITY	Important	Not Important
LIKABILITY	Important	Not Important
LOVE	Important	Not Important
SPIRITUALITY/RELIGION	Important	Not Important

PART 3: Favorites

List your favorites (be specific).

FOOD:

SONG:

BOOK:

MOVIE:

TV SHOW:

CITY:

SEASON:

COLOR:

PIECE OF CLOTHING:

SMELL:

ANIMAL:

SOUND:

SCHOOL SUBJECT:

PLACE:

PERSON (historical or living):

PART 4: Describe Yourself

Circle all words/phrases that apply to you:

SHY	OUTGOING
OUTDOOR TYPE	INDOOR TYPE
POSITIVE	NEGATIVE
PARTY PERSON	COUCH POTATO
HOMEBODY	LEADER
FOLLOWER	MOODY
CALM	SILLY
HAPPY	SAD
RELAXED	ENERGETIC
INTELLECTUAL	CLEVER
NEAT	MESSY
FUNNY	HONEST
SNEAKY	DISHONEST
OPEN-MINDED	JUDGMENTAL
CARING	CREATIVE
PRACTICAL	WILD
CAREFUL	WELL-LIKED
ARTISTIC	LAZY
OPINIONATED	IMAGINATIVE
REALISTIC	DRAMATIC
STREETWISE	TOLERANT
HARD-WORKING	SPONTANEOUS
STRONG	BRAVE
CURIOUS	QUIET
CHATTY	DARK
SUNNY	DISAPPOINTING
HOPEFUL	UNDERSTANDING
KIND	BORED
DIFFICULT	COMPLICATED
SWEET	POWERFUL
MACHO	ENTHUSIASTIC
GIRLY	INSECURE
LUCKY	PICKY
DISADVANTAGED	FRIENDLY
GOSSIPY	ANGRY
SECRETIVE	WISHY-WASHY
INDEPENDENT	GEEKY
WEAK	COOL
NURTURING	ANNOYING
REBELLIOUS	GOOD

PART 5: Truth/Dreams

If I die tomorrow, people will remember me as a:

One thing that really annoys me is:

My worst habit is:

I'm really scared of:

My parents think I'm:

When I grow up, I want to be*:

Superpower I'd most like to have:

The thing I'd most like to change about myself is:

My greatest talent is:

I'd most like to travel to:

Three professions I'd like to try:

The title for the story of my life would be:

* If your character is an adult, what is your character's job and does he or she enjoy it?

PLAYWRIGHT'S CHECKLIST

Does my play have:

☐ **Conflict?**

If everyone gets along, not much happens! It's important to have conflict in any play, comedy, or drama.

☐ **Character development?**

Do the characters change at all in the course of the play for better or worse? It's interesting to the audience to see some variety in character. We all act differently in different situations, so it makes sense for a character to become more complex when he or she is faced with conflicts.

☐ **Plot twists?**

What could be more exciting than being surprised by a plot twist you hadn't expected?

☐ **Believable dialogue?**

Even if the characters are strange and out-of-this-world, make sure the dialogue sounds something like the way people actually speak to one another. Any character voices you create must remain consistent throughout. For example, if a character is very intellectual and proper, having them say "I ain't gonna go" is going to seem very out of place.

☐ A strong sense of place and time?

Especially when you don't have a big set and costumes, it's important to make the play's setting clear.

☐ Characters you can relate to?

Every play has at least one character the audience can understand and sympathize with. A good way to create conflict is to put this "normal" character in the path of another character that is odd, otherworldly, or downright horrible!

SCENE ELEMENTS WORKSHEET

Answer these questions for each scene you do.

WHO: (Who are you?)

WHERE: (Where are you?)

WHEN: (Is this the past, present, or future? Day or night?)

WHY: (Why are you where you are?)

OBJECTIVE: (What do you want?)

ACTIONS: (What do you do to get what you want? For example, beg, flatter, pressure, and so on.)

CHARACTER TRAITS: (What are you like as a person?)

RELATIONSHIP: (What are your relationships to the other characters?)

OBSTACLES: (What or who stands in the way of your objective?)

EXPLORATION GAMES

Draw a picture of your character(s).

Improvise a scene before the play begins or after it ends.

Dress as your character(s) to see how it changes your behavior.

Make the scene or play into a musical or an opera.

Listen closely to everyone around you during a scene.

Try to make your acting partners respond to your behavior.

Lead with a different body part: in other words, change which part of your body enters the room first and pulls you forward when you walk. Leading with your nose can make you seem pompous, leading with the top of your head can make you seem insecure, etc.

Change the speed/rhythm at which you speak or move.

Decide who you like and who you don't like in the scene; don't be afraid to show it.

Change your volume (whisper or speak out loudly).

Make your voice higher or lower in pitch.

Notice who's taller and who's shorter than you in the scene; let this affect you.

Change your accent.

Sit down with another actor to make up your characters' past lives together.

Do an activity you think your character might do.

Do a chore around the house the way your character might do it.

Write a diary entry, a letter of complaint, or a personal ad as your character.

Come up with a gesture that your character does habitually.

THE AUTHOR

Kristen Dabrowski is an actress, writer, acting teacher, and director. She received her MFA from The Oxford School of Drama in Oxford, England. The actor's life has taken her all over the United States and England. Her other books, published by Smith and Kraus, include *111 Monologues for Middle School Actors Volume 1, The Ultimate Audition Book for Teens 3, 20 Ten-Minute Plays for Teens,* and the *Teens Speak* series. Currently, she lives in the world's smallest apartment in New York City. You can contact the author at monologue madness@yahoo.com.